A HISTORY OF ANGLING

A HISTORY OF
ANGLING

CHARLES F. WATERMAN

WINCHESTER PRESS

Tulsa, Oklahoma

Library of Congress Cataloging in Publication Data
Waterman, Charles F.
History of American angling.

Bibliography: p. 243
1. Fishing—United States—History.   2. Fishing
—History.   I. Title.
SH421.W37   799.1'2'0973   81-10384
ISBN 0-87691-343-5   AACR2

Published by Winchester Press
1421 South Sheridan Road
Post Office Box 1260
Tulsa, Oklahoma 74101

Printed in the United States of America

1 2 3 4 5 85 84 83 82 81

For my wife Debie, who is really more interested in
this afternoon's fishing than in all that
old stuff.

A FISHING HISTORY

Let me tell you about this book so you'll know if you really want to read it.

I've written a history of sport fishing, mainly in America. Since sport fishing evolved from subsistence fishing I've included some notes on commercial operations, but I made no effort at telling the entire story of that.

The account of early sport angling deals mainly with British and American developments. American angling has been most varied and generally the most innovative. Traditions came from Britain.

A fault with histories is that they are written by historians, scholars who become immersed in academic offshoots and complex conclusions. It's hard to keep from heading off on a tangent, for a thousand pages could be written about fishhooks and several thousand about old bamboo rods. Other authors have done these things well and comprehensively. I have shamelessly lifted information from them.

It is tempting to wade too deeply into the words of Izaak Walton and Dame Juliana. I haven't ignored them, but their works have been dissected through the centuries and I leave their literary analysis to specialists. I use them only to help tell the fishing story and if I appear a bit irreverent now and then I am sure they would understand.

I have tried to trace our popular gamefish from pre-history—briefly—and have managed to drag myself away from pre-historic man without overdoing his fishing experiences. This is my personal weakness and I hanker to delve into the archaeology of the business, a field in which I am a rank amateur with the amateur's naive enthusiasm for what happened a million years ago. I'm experienced in this restraint because I went through it in writing *Fishing In America* a few years back, an account with a different and more disciplined approach.

I guess the heaviest emphasis is on the period from 1850 to the 1980s, simply because it was during that period our present methods and equipment were developed.

I have tried to handle the equipment angle with reason, aware that the details of rod, reel and lure construction can get out of hand. To the disgust of some learned collectors (whom I hold in awe) I have not cut a very fine line in the minute changes through various models of rods and reels but I have tried to run down the important ones. This book is about fishing rather than equipment, although the two are inseparable.

There's a strange polarization between trout and salmon anglers and black bass fishermen, neither group seeming to know much about the other's heroes and traditions. The "literary" writing has been mainly about trout and trout fishing, much of it in moody flights of rather flowery prose. Then came the nuts and bolts bass writers and their insistence upon a backwoods dialect wherever possible (even if the speaker or writer holds a Ph.D. in English) and a scorn for tradition or flattering terms applied to bass. Both groups have histories and I have tried to be fair.

The saltwater sportsmen are the newest clan with their own salty traditions, mostly within the past hundred years.

So I tried to put it in one package.

Charles F. Waterman

ACKNOWLEDGMENTS

Among those who helped to put this history together, I am especially indebted to Frank Woolner of the high surf; Warren Shepard, angling historian; Roland Jarrard, who collects things I never heard of; Jim Martenhoff, who knows where boats came from; Paul Schullery of the Museum of American Fly Fishing; those efficient folks working with E.K. Harry of the International Game Fish Association; officers of the American Casting Association; George Anderson of Yellowstone Angler; and people like Fred Terwilliger of Dan Bailey's Fly Shop who were willing to lend me rare old books.

CONTENTS

xi

CHAPTER ONE

WHO FISHES?

Fishing for fun is a strange business. For a visitor from outer space, the sight of a man playing a fish with rod and reel would surely be one of the most puzzling spectacles of Earth.

One of the most popular recreations of all time has been elaborately contrived through the centuries. The equipment has been developed constantly, but has followed some frequently changing rules so as not to take too much advantage of the fish.

Sport fishing is so varied and its practitioners are such a motley crew that the rules vary from river to river and from boat to boat. Fact is that fishing for sport involves carefully imposed personal handicaps. That's what separates it from commercial fishing and subsistence fishing; nets and electric shocking equipment are far more practical than ultra-light tackle and artificial lures.

Personal angling codes, of course, are what make fishing a sport, and if it weren't for them our methods and equipment would never have developed at all. We have to understand some of these individual rules in order to trace the history. Ever since the rod was invented (or discovered) fishermen have been faced with a choice each time a new tool is perfected.

A large share of the world's anglers have restricted themselves to artificial lures. This makes fishing more fun, an added challenge. This does not mean artificial lure fishing always requires more skill than bait fishing. I have seen a flyfishing purist momentarily nonplussed when a bait angler said he believed in doing things nature's way and felt the addition of artificial things was unfair.

Charles Ernst is a superb saltwater angler with a background in commerical fishing. Although he uses natural bait at times, he prefers artificials when given a choice. He summed up one viewpoint succinctly:

Shakespeare "Revolution" lure (circa 1902) was made of aluminum and resembles some sort of space vehicle when viewed at close range.

Who Fishes?

"I like to fool the fish myself. God makes shrimp. I make jigs."

Westerners have until recently been considered rather crude in fly fishing for trout, probably because their trout were more plentiful and easier to catch than those of the Catskills or Britain. Recently I showed a Western angler a delicately built beetle, formed by a true master in the East. It employed a wisp of cork for flotation, not unusual on some Eastern streams, notably Pennsylvania's Letort, a highly "technical" water.

When he saw the cork, my friend showed some embarrassment.

"I'm sure it will catch trout," he said, "but I use flies made only of feather and hair. If it has anything else it is not a fly."

Extend this to the nymph fisherman who will not add weight to the hook. Extend it to the fisherman who will not cast except to fish he has seen, only "fishing the rise." Now extend it to the fisherman who will not add wire to his leader when fishing toothy saltwater fish. Consider the bass fisherman who will use only surface lures, the trout angler who will fish only dry flies and the offshore record seeker who stipulates that he gaff his own fish.

These things are very important because they laid the routes of fishing history—not merely a series of improved ways of catching fish, but a complex network of codes and variant objectives. People were not satisfied merely to catch fish. They insisted upon catching them in certain ways, demonstrating certain skills and enjoying certain equipment. A cynic could say they are training fish.

Somewhere along the way there was a move to establish use of light-test line as a measure of skill, and in an extreme instance, a fisherman might not care how he hooked his quarry, but takes pride in his prowess in playing it to submission with the lightest possible connection. Now we have fishermen competing with the fish *and* with one another. This called for special qualities in tackle.

Casting in itself has been a game, although casting competition has not attracted a great deal of attention in recent years. In one respect the casting tournament has been to fishing what the racetrack has been to automobiles. That's where the equipment developed. Some people won't fish if it doesn't involve casting—another pride in personal skill.

So we'll tell not only *how* fishing developed, but *why* it developed. We'll follow these things from the beginning, but there are some markers of angling history to be noted first.

3

As a sport, fishing started slowly, for it lacked the glamour of hunting. It was natural for a public hero of 2000 years ago to take his recreation in a warlike sport. Some of the early hunting expeditions were truly military, employing thousands of soldiers if a warrior king sought venison or grouse. By contrast, angling was "meditative," an overworked word but hard to replace in describing the passive joys of lolling by a trout stream. In those times a fishing boat far at sea was certainly not there for fun.

Izaak Walton in his angler's role was hardly a heroic figure as compared to the great hunters of his time (17th century), and might even have been considered an undesirable loafer. He probably added little to the mechanics of sport fishing, charming though his bucolic observations have been through the centuries. His friend, Charles Cotton, who appeared with flyfishing instruction in later editions by Walton, was the technician.

Up to that point the development of fly fishing wasn't well re-

Thousands of firms have been involved in fishing tackle;
few have survived from the 1890s.
(Photo courtesy of The Museum of American Fly Fishing, Inc.)

4

corded, although *The Boke of St. Albans* appeared in 1496, presenting an assortment of flies and a passable rod. The "boke" has been belabored by generations of scholars and the fishing section in it is generally attributed to Dame Juliana Berners, the prioress of a nunnery. Anyway, flies had been used for hundreds of years before that, whether for sport or simply as a good way of getting a seafood dinner we don't know.

Through any neat chronology of angling development run the unaltered methods of antiquity, still used by primitive people and sometimes preferred by thoroughly modern folk. For example, I correspond with a "swimfisherman" who is something of a world traveler and has practiced his sport in many waters, often far offshore. Not to be confused with a spearfisherman, this sportsman swims while trolling a lure behind him, a method far too elementary for Izaak Walton, and probably a bit hairy even for aboriginal food seekers.

The handline is certainly associated with primitive fishing but it is not necessarily dangled straight down from a gunwale or worked from a cliff. I have watched a Mexican handliner turn off his Evinrude and throw a bait with deadly accuracy from loops held in his hand or coiled on his deck. At surprising distances he could intercept cruising fish already sighted in shallow water. While few sport anglers choose to employ such tactics, it is hard to say it is anything but sporting.

In Argentina, as in many parts of the world, a trout fisherman does his spinfishing with a gallon can and modern fishing line. He wraps line around the can the way it goes around a spinning reel's spool and then whirls his lure about his head, paying off line by simply aiming his tin can in the direction the lure is flying. He retrieves with a flexible wrist and a little sleight-of-hand.

These methods require skill, a commodity much desired in sport fishing, but they lack one of the ingredients essential to most anglers where enjoyment is concerned—fine equipment. A survey shows that use of equipment is one of the main attractions of outdoor sport for *most* of us. Pride of possession in fishing gear ranges from collecting the finest split bamboo rods to owning complex electronic fish-finding apparatus. I'm reaching into the field of psychology but it's doubtful if sport angling could ever have reached its current station without fine equipment. Many of the current crop of bass-fishing enthusiasts, for example, would be doing something else if it were not for the wonderfully gadgeted bass boat. It was gadgetry status that caused an enormous surge in bass fishing in the 60s.

Fly casting has been an aristocrat of angling in Europe, especially England, since before 1700. Skipping the earliest developments, we begin with rods that could be taken down and were frequently made of more than one material. They could be fastened together or spliced by wrapping matched diagonal cuts.

Call it "casting," but as to when the rod began to throw the line rather than just swinging it, we simply can't tell. Those very long and very heavy rods of 300 years ago certainly did not have the action of modern rods that are matched to carefully shaped lines of numbered weights. Since the early lines had fairly large diameter they were probably "cast" after a fashion, but the casting distance was a product of the length of the rod, and most were operated with both

Herbert Hoover was perhaps the most enthusiastic of our angling Presidents. The Museum of American Fly Fishing has his Hardy rod and reel, as well as fly box and leader tin. The center picture was taken in Yellowstone Park in the 1920s; the ranger is Park Superintendent Horace Albright. The smaller picture was taken in Idaho. (Photo courtesy of The Museum of American Fly Fishing, Inc.)

hands. It was with the more advanced fly rods that the reel was moved down to the butt for one-hand operation.

Only a few years ago there were many Atlantic salmon fishermen who insisted upon the long, two-handed rod, a weapon that now is generally used only under special conditions. Only a very long rod can put a fly over extremely swift and unwadeable rivers if there are tall standing waves waiting to wither an ordinary cast. Don't downrate these enormous rods until you have seen a British caster roll a length of line or have watched a tournament competitor in the "salmon fly distance" event.

True casting from turning spool reels, throwing a lure or bait as the weight rather than the line itself, has been largely an American development and took two directions at first: black bass fishing and surf fishing for striped bass. Freshwater casting evidently came first and the Kentucky reel is recognized as father of the casting tool. Although collectors often favor fly tackle, Kentucky reels are avidly sought in attics and garages by ardent scholars. The reels' monetary value is not yet well established but great finds are becoming fewer as years go by. The day of the $5 original Meek in mint condition with leather case has passed, but I can remember it.

Modern reels cast better, but the first Kentuckies (around 1800) were handmade by jewelers and built to endure. Strangely, they were first intended for bait fishing, although artificial flies were already traditional for trout and salmon. The black bass, an American provincial, had no tradition and had not yet followed the railroads to the frontier. In 1800, few Americans were interested in hauling bass fry about in wooden buckets.

The spools of the Kentucky reels were heavy and "slow," cursed by a "flywheel action" that would have made an accurate wrist-snapping cast impossible. Rods were long, and a soft lob was the ideal way of presenting a live bait for the early bass fisherman, a sort of bumpkin of the sports fishing scene.

Fly fishing for bass is much older than plugcasting, being a minor natural offshoot of trout and salmon fishing. It was a long time before the bass plug was recognized. By the time the plug was called by that name, rather than "artificial minnow," the turning-spool, multiplying Kentucky reel had been used for so long to throw live bait to largemouth bass that it was permanently associated with "baitcasting." This confusing term stays with freshwater fishing to this day, even while earnest well-meaners try to change its name to "plugcasting" (which, of course, isn't completely correct either. The rigs are used to throw all sorts of artificials.)

Evidently the casting method is an American product. The multiplying reel had been around a long time before the Kentucky reel, but if it was actually used in casting, that part of its task was not considered important. British historians, speaking freely of the multiplier, simply do not stress it as a caster.

Invention of the "plug" is credited to Jim Heddon. Almost 100 years after the casting reel was first built was the beginning of modern "plugcasting," whether the new lure was novel enough to be considered a separate form or not.

Historians thresh helplessly in terminology. The term *spinning* was (I think) first used to mean retrieving a natural or artificial minnow so

Modern materials have made inshore saltwater fishing simple.
This angler has hooked a small tarpon from a tiny aluminum pram.

that it spun as it came through the water. Spinners were also spoon-shaped or propeller-shaped attractions preceding or following lures. When fixed-reel casting came to America it was called spinning. A highly popular bass lure of the 1970s and 1980s is called a *spinnerbait.*

Angling in the early 19th century was hardly big news, especially in America, where it developed along several different routes at the same time. In the South, Kentucky bass fishermen were casting bait delicately with simple but light rods. In the North and East everything but fly rods appeared to be true poles until late in the century. Fly fishing methods and equipment were borrowed from England until American rod makers came on the scene with their versions of split bamboo.

Puritanical American colonists had taken a dim view of any sort of sport. Fishing was considered a trivial waste of time. Anybody who spent a great deal of his life at it was considered a loafer or worse, and even after those attitudes began to erode it was some time before fishing got into print.

Americans made some good rods but they didn't start the "rent and glue" process. Split bamboo had been used in England for some time to make short sections of rods. Americans came on pretty strong after about 1860 and won some casting contests against the British somewhat later. The British had "rent and glue" sections in some of their rods from about 1800 on. It seems the bamboo splitting business started because of efforts to use the best parts of the cane and discard the bad pieces. Cane was glued and wrapped together in many ways, sometimes in two strips, then in three, four and six strips. At first it was only the tips that were split and laminated, but about 1848 Samuel Phillippi of Easton, Pennsylvania, a gunsmith and violin maker, produced the first complete American split bamboo rod.

Eventually, the most popular construction was to be in six strips, although some four-strip rods were made and used for more than 100 years. They feel different but they work.

At first the biggest problem was glue and a need for a lot of silk wrappings. Fishermen argued about wrappings and how much they helped or hindered rod action. When waterproof glue was developed much later, the copious wrappings began to disappear, and split bamboo rods of the 1980s had little thread except for guides and ferrules.

Tradition was hard to live down, and even after waterproof glue arrived, the more expensive rods often carried extra silk for cosmetic reasons. The colors were pretty, even if the glue was working.

For a long time the black bass angler was something of an outcast among traditional sport fishermen. The smallmouth was caught occasionally by trout and salmon fishermen on fly tackle but the largemouth, having a more southern range, lacked national notice for many years.

Today, when black bass fishing is by far the most publicized angling sport of all in the United States, and when the ubiquitous bass boat as a status symbol has bolstered the boating industry, and when black bass tournament winners are the best known of all anglers, it might come as a shock to read this quotation from a fishing history written by Charles Chenevix Trench, published in England in 1974:

"Many fine sporting fish—the black bass for instance, the mahseer and the Nile perch—are barely mentioned *(here)* because they require no great novelties of angling method."

This is no criticism of the Trench history at all, simply a demonstration of the polarization that exists between various angling groups, divided by quarry and method. Two hundred years ago this situation was enormously magnified. A British fly fisherman for Atlantic salmon had never even *heard* of a black bass and many American trout fishermen hadn't either.

One of the first true invasions of salt water by sport anglers came just after the Civil War in America in the surf fishing for striped bass along the North Atlantic coast. Up until that time ocean fishing was almost entirely a matter of collecting food. Trolling for bluefish with handlines and small sailing craft had long been a sort of family outing along the coast, but surf fishing was accommodated by good casting reels and efficient rods. The reels had undoubtedly been influenced by the Kentucky multiplier.

Striped bass clubs were made up of Eastern industrialists, and their traces are still found along the coast. Their clubhouses were substantial, and "stands" were built on the rocky shores. Exceptional skill was developed in casting to feeding fish. Fishermen even lashed themselves to platforms in the face of crushing seas. The clubs faded when the striper disappeared temporarily as the century ended. Almost invariably, saltwater angling has grown from freshwater meth-

10

ods. It is very rare that a saltwater method moves inland. The jig did go to fresh water from the salt, but it may be that it was first used in fresh water by primitive fishermen.

From 1870 until about 1920 (arbitrary dates but we have to use some kind of framework) was an especially important period because of a worldwide stocking of fish species due to improved transportation.

In America, the black bass was distributed across the country by rail and adapted efficiently to its new range, later becoming the number one game species. The Eastern brook trout went to appropriate waters. The rainbow trout, originally found only on the West Coast, went to the Midwest and the East.

The brown trout came to America from Britain and Germany and it, as well as the rainbow, was planted in South America, New Zealand and Australia as well as in dozens of other areas.

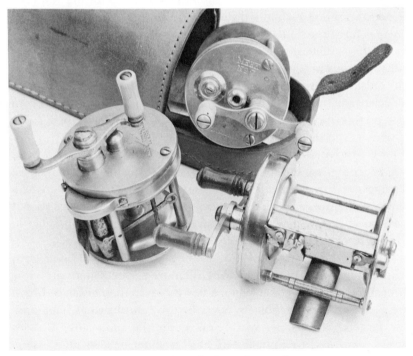

Some antique baitcasting reels.
The one in the background is a Meek in the original leather case.
The other two show early level-wind mechanisms.

11

The striped bass, the East's top saltwater gamefish, went to the West Coast and prospered, and so did shad taken from the East Coast rivers.

Not all of the introductions were satisfactory. Billed as a super-fish for sport and food, the German carp was sloshed into American waters where it immediately competed with native fish, degraded many lakes and rivers, and established itself as a permanent curse.

American trout fishing had a poor reputation in its earlier days. The visiting Europeans, accustomed to the difficult brown trout, found the naive wild brookie too easy and American fishing methods notably crude. When the colonists first arrived, the Atlantic salmon were too plentiful to be sporting, but they soon became too scarce to be sporting. United States salmon fishing deteriorated until around 1970, when it began the long road back—with numerous detours.

Where trout were concerned the Americans had always followed England's lead, though at a distance. The Europeans had been using dry flies for some time while the Americans were still slopping crude wets before gullible brookies. When they acquired the selective brown the Americans needed more advanced methods. Theodore Gordon of the Catskills brought the true dry fly from England after correspondence with Frederic Halford, the English master of the dry. From then on there was a cult of advanced American trout fishermen, some of whom even bowed to tradition.

Until nearly 1900 the inshore species of saltwater fish had been largely ignored except for the bluefish and striped bass. When some northern sportsmen finally discovered Florida's tarpon there was a flurry of attempts at landing the Silver King with heavy tackle. Then it was found that with a little restraint the tarpon was vulnerable to freshwater gear, including the fly rod.

Although the "party boat" or "fishing excursion boat" had been around for some time, the swift offshore "sportfisherman" was unheard of until after 1900 when a few very rich men began to prowl the world's seas for monsters never before considered as hook-and-line targets. The fishing world was never the same after Charles Holder caught a well-publicized bluefin tuna in 1898 off Catalina Island. Zane Grey did much to promote offshore angling.

In the meantime, baitcasting had developed to an art in America, although it was almost completely ignored elsewhere. The stationary spool reel, in turn, was a stranger in America until after World War II, although it had been widely used in Europe in one form or another for more than 20 years.

Fishing lines are simple in use but of complex construction. They probably began with vines in pre-history. Horsehair was the prime component during Dame Juliana's day. Silk was used in many forms and was the top freshwater material shortly after 1900. Linen was used in salt water.

It is impossible to learn when the fly line's weight began to work the rod and to truly shoot line, but silk fly lines were built in numerous conformations in the early 1900s. Before World War II nylon mono-filament had its beginnings but it was not efficient until the late 40s. Monofilament came with modern spinning tackle, and some say it is what made the spinning reel work, but the stationary spool was good with braided line, too.

Already of age elsewhere, spinning was tried in the United States in the 30s but didn't make its revolutionary conquest until after the troops came home from Europe and Asia. It may not be the most aesthetic form of fishing, but it brought casting to everyone. No longer was it necessary to educate a thumb or learn the vagaries of the fly caster's aerial loop.

Fly fishermen had long abused their medium by using lures just a little heavier than their rods wanted—spinnerfly combinations, mid-get wooden plugs and small spoons. The spinning gear took over these lures immediately. Slightly heavier spinning rods worked with baitcasting plugs and longer-heavier spinning gear went to the surf, where it very nearly shouldered aside the conventional surf real.

Spinfishermen set up their own organizations and stated frankly that other kinds of tackle were outdated. They even equipped their spinning outfits with "casting bubbles" and used them with dry flies. They went to ultra-light and for a time "threadline" was a common term. Trout fishermen went to small streams with lines testing two pounds or less and cast tiny attractors no bigger than conventional wet flies.

Spinning reels were made in closed-face or "pushbutton" types and the British, especially the Australians, were fond of great salt water reels that would turn from standard spinning position to conventional silhouette for retrieve. It looked as if fly fishing and plugging would fade away.

But there were some upheavals in the other disciplines. For a long time tournament casters had used some freespooling baitcasting reels of freshwater dimensions, but not many had been used for light fishing. Surf reels had freespooled for some time. At first the plugging reels began to appear with faster spools and nylon gears, but when the Swedish Ambassadeur freespool reel arrived baitcasting began a comeback. Other manufacturers built fast freespoolers using a variety of mechanical inventions. Baitcasting was coming back.

Things happened in fly casting too. Before the war bamboo had been the undisputed leader in rod material, despite some really fine hollow steel rods such as the True Temper of the American Fork and Hoe Company. When fiberglass arrived with the Howald process in the foreground, good rod action became less expensive and highly durable, and along came fly lines built by new processes with plastics that did not require the care of silk and could be made in any profile.

Steelhead fishermen did more for fly *casting* than any other fishing group. They needed long casts over the plunging torrents of the West Coast and they organized casting clubs. Along came the "shooting head," a short section of heavy material with monofilament "running line" that added greatly to casting range. The shooting heads were built to scour the bottom gravels of steelhead rivers and later moved to trout lakes and rivers, and even into salt water. Fly fishing could never displace spinning tackle but the purist could give a good account of himself in competition with spinning.

At first the new glass rods could not compete with split cane, but they became better rapidly. Once the processes were well learned the glass rod's action could be even more predictable than that of bamboo. Bamboo began to lose its place in heavy fishing, although it continued to hold the connoisseur's allegiance on small trout streams. It still does, although a bamboo tarpon rod is now a curiosity.

Along came graphite.

Like other new materials, graphite suffered growing pains and breakage. At first it appeared mostly in fly rods but then it was used in spinning and plugcasting rods, sometimes in combination with fiberglass, much as early bamboo had been mixed with ash or green heart. It became a fine medium for rod construction—great power with light weight.

Then came boron, and the jury is still out.

Bonefish took the light tackle angler's artificial and sizzled it out to sea. A true bonefish craze began in the 50s when it was found they could be caught on flies and light spinning tackle. The true craze and its attendant literary hyperbole gradually faded, although bonefishing remained a class sport. After catching tarpon and bonefish, the fly fisherman decided he could handle anything. He very nearly has.

The cobia, the striper and the dolphin were caught on flies. Then came the billfish, and on the West Coast the steelheader found he could handle big salmon.

The outrigger and the improved depth sounder allowed true sport-fishermen to work offshore. In the 50s began the "fishing machine," usually an outboard, that brought Zane Grey's distant combers within range of the angler of more modest means.

In Texas, the Skeeter was designed, a rather unusual decked-in fishing craft that went particularly well with an electric motor for shore-line casting. The bass boat. It became a status symbol in the South and then the Midwest, it grew and became a high-speed fishing laboratory with more comforts than home and an almost indecent capacity for studying the black bass in his home.

When the Tennessee Valley Authority built the big power dams they stilled forever the black bass rivers, but the big lakes soon supported more bass than the rivers ever had—and more fishermen too.

An insurance man named Ray Scott set up an experimental bass tournament and began a highly profitable craze that swept through the marine industry (bass boats), through the clothing factories (jump suits and dressy life jackets) and through the tackle plants (better and more expensive everything). Fisheries biologists found that the world wanted more bass and was willing to pay the bill.

Bass professionals wrote their own books, directed their own television shows and endorsed a spate of plastic worms, crankbaits, spinnerbaits, bass boats and tackle boxes. The public loved the whole thing and joined bass clubs.

For the most part the serious trout angler pretended not to notice. He had discovered new techniques with nymphs and spoke Latin when the subject turned to entomology. Catch-and-release was his religion and a new era of trout angling was born.

In 30 years angling had come farther than in the preceding 3,000.

CHAPTER TWO

IN THE BEGINNING

Truly ancient history of fishes is usually glossed over or turned into a subject in itself. Let's do neither, but look at it in the light of how it has affected sport fishing, and where gamefish came from.

After a look at evolution—and lack of it—through millions of years a modern angler may be a little surprised at his own selection of a "game" fish. The ones he has chosen to pursue are not necessarily the most intelligent or the most highly evolved. Some of them have changed little through the eons.

His requirements are often quickly summarized. A gamefish by some standards must be willing to take an artificial lure. All agree it should make something of a fight on appropriate tackle. Some say it should jump and some insist it must be good to eat, but many of the most prized trophies lack more than one of these criteria. Certainly some of the finest gamefish have rather limited intelligence, even by fish standards, and the trouts, sought by some of the most sophisticated of all anglers, are said to be pretty well down on the scale of intellects.

This makes absolutely no difference in a fish's sporting qualities for if it is difficult to catch by the method with which the fisherman handicaps himself, we say it is "smart." A brown trout is hard to fool with a tiny dry fly, but if a catfish is more intelligent, who cares? If we don't look at it this way we find ourselves "rating" fish, which is silly.

Evolution is not necessarily in a continuing direction. For example, it's believed the first life on earth began at some indeterminate time in the extensive warm seas. Then certain creatures "evolved" into land animals by forsaking the seas. But it seems that a few million years later some of them "evolved" back again. Land animals aren't necessarily more intelligent than water creatures. A porpoise can outthink an opossum any day.

Evolution, much of it seemingly by pure chance, has provided a wide selection of gamefish for America. Natural barriers have caused various species to take different courses, as in the case of those close relatives the Atlantic salmon and the rainbow trout. At one time, it is believed, they were the same fish, but when an ocean north of Canada got too cold, part of them went to the Pacific and part to the Atlantic. It is fun to throw these conclusions around when you don't have to prove them.

We don't know just how evolution went a million years ago and we aren't even sure how it's headed now. The steelhead is a rainbow that goes to sea and returns to spawn, and experts say all rainbows have some of the seagoing trait. Are the rainbows turning into ocean fish from fresh water or are they turning into freshwater fish from salt water?

The beaver is a pretty high form of mammal but he has a funny tail and spends much of his life in the water. Is his evolution toward the water or the dry land? Obviously he's somewhere in between at present.

None of this helps you select a fly or find a school of bluefish but it can give a clue as to how America's fisheries started, developed and occasionally fell on hard times.

Since most of the earlier forms of fish did not have bone skeletons, they made poor fossils; their frameworks were made of cartilage. Today's sharks, chimaeras, skates and rays have that structure. Bowfins and sturgeons have skeletons that are part bone and part cartilage.

Like a vision from the past the alligator gar,
one of the "ancient fishes," has brought his armor plate
down through the ages.
This one, shot with bow and arrow, is held by Kevin Brown.
(Photo from The Ken Brown Guide to Bowfishing)

The popular viewpoint is that the bony skeleton means a more advanced form. Strangely, the "more advanced" forms of life haven't necessarily been the ones to survive longest, and some of the most elemental fish have continued to thrive while more "advanced" species have disappeared. And some of the most elemental creatures have incredibly acute senses. The shark, for example, is little changed from pre-history but has almost supernatural abilities in detecting food at a distance.

Any sport fisherman who studies illustrations of ancient fishes will have an eerie feeling of looking behind the scenes. Working from the fossils, skillful artists undoubtedly can come very close to what the original looked like. As you examine the pictures you'll see a number of fish that look vaguely or strongly familiar, even though they may have been much larger or much smaller than their modern descendants.

Any tarpon fisherman who examines a picture of Portheus will have the instant feeling that the artist has been drawing a tarpon and made a few errors. Portheus, a fish that lived when reptilian giants covered Earth, was 14 feet long, but if reduced to scale would have drawn little attention in a school of modern Silver Kings. The tarpon, a rather elemental member of the herring family, has outlasted the mammoth and the saber-toothed tiger.

Like some other modern fish, the tarpon has elemental lungs which account for its rolling on the surface for air. Perhaps most gamefish are "higher forms," but they're hardly more efficient.

Let's look at a few bare evolutionary facts. It is tempting to enlarge endlessly on them, but they give us the really essential background just as they are.

Fossilized creatures from 500 million years ago have been found. That was the Cambrian period and from then on through the next 175 million years life existed in warm waters. Probably the first vertebrate fishes came afterward when the mountain ranges had formed, and freshwater streams and lakes were present. Most of our gamefish belong to the order *Teleostei,* fully vertebrate.

Experts say big sea mammals such as porpoises, seals and whales evolved from land animals, giving up their legs for fins. Then we get back to our friends the beaver and the otter, and possibly the muskrat. We don't know where they're headed. We end with the conclusion that evolution succeeds or fails because of changes in habitat, and it is obvious that it can veer off or even retreat when conditions warrant.

There are 40,000 kinds of fish. The term "evolution" can apply to almost any change from generation to generation. The most startling thing about present fish species and sub-species is how they can adapt and change within a few years. Fish managers can erase a strain of fish or they can change its form and lifestyle.

A good reason why aquatic giants have survived when more advanced land animals have become extinct is the supportive quality of water. With the firm support of water a creature can become very large and maneuverable with very little skeletal support. On land, the physical structure must be more rigid, more "advanced."

Some observers point to the comparative ease of migration for sea creatures on a planet that was largely water. If one section of the oceans became too cold, its residents could move to warmer water. A land animal might be cut off by water from extensive migrations. Birds could migrate temporarily or permanently for great distances.

Today, although much more is made of the long migrations of birds, oceanic travels by fish are just as impressive and their homing instincts just as accurate. In fact, the senses that bring anadromous fish back to the creeks of their birth after years at sea may be more spectacular than the instincts that work for birds. It's unlikely that fish can make use of celestial navigation, and depths of the open sea have no landmarks as we recognize them. The mystery of fish and their travels makes fishing more fun but can complicate fish management. We have finally learned that the oceans must be managed.

The adaptability of fishes sometimes seems to overwhelm their most outstanding characteristics. The Atlantic salmon, for example, returns to its native stream to spawn after a varying number of years at sea, and much is made of this marvel of nature, the oceanic tour seeming to be an essential part of the fish's welfare. But we also have the landlocked Atlantic salmon, evidently the same fish, that has learned to reproduce and thrive without access to salt water at all. Some of the landlocks have been taken from their Northeastern habitat and transplanted successfully in the West.

At the moment the most heralded advancements in fish management involve moving anadromous fish (those spending part of their lives in salt and part in fresh water) into completely freshwater habitat, where some of them reproduce. The fact that others do not reproduce is a boon in some cases. Without reproduction, quantity control can be complete.

Examples of the move to "all-fresh" water are the striped bass, the Atlantic salmon, the Pacific salmon and the snook. The snook, a tropical and subtropical gamefish, is especially interesting because it is believed that some snook never go into fresh water at all. It is possible this is true of some striped bass.

These moves from fresh to salt water, or the other way around, show an association with far-reaching possibilities. All of the trouts and chars have representatives living part of the time in salty or at least brackish water. At first glance it would appear the vast expanses of ocean could accommodate an endless supply of game and commercial species, but the fact is that most oceanic fish live on the edges of the sea in habitat that is as much endangered and harder to control than inland waters.

In the case of the Atlantic salmon, seagoing fish grow much larger than the landlocks. The largest numbers of other species are also often ocean goers, but this is not a hard and fast rule. Brackish water is the most fertile of all, and the oceans are generally acknowledged to produce more of what a gamefish needs than does fresh water.

But in general usage, "brackish" is an indefinite term. We think of it as being somewhere between salt and fresh, but that covers a wide range of salinity. There are brackish water black bass and freshwater striped bass. Most species have great tolerance for living, if not reproducing, where salinity is concerned. They may or may not require a considerable period for gradual adaptation. For that matter, some parts of the true ocean are much saltier than other parts.

So much for a general look at fish. Let's look at early fishermen.

Man had been eating fish for a long time, I suppose, before any kind of fishing became sport. Many early cultures were based upon seafood but there were others that evidently did not consider fish edible, even though living very near to productive waters. There were fish cultures and hunting cultures, and some of the most progressive made use of both land and sea for food. Probably some tribes grew away from fishing while others gravitated toward it.

A sport fisherman probably feels that the fruition of angling progress is the dry fly, the spinnerbait or the plastic worm. More practical observers could consider it the use of electric shocking devices, the longline of offshore commercial operators, or fish finding with electronic devices.

Early angling history is skimpy because fishing lacked the romantic appeal of hunting, as it was generally associated with war. American sport angling came from western Europe and more principally Great Britain. Our knowledge of Asiatic angling is scarce because works translated into Western languages were concerned with more important topics. There was no indication early in the game that recreational angling would ever become a worldwide passion. So we Americans have to tread a little gingerly concerning the very earliest rod and line sport fishing. We never did find out much about it.

Subsistence fishing is not so mysterious and the developments are traced pretty accurately. We know that early tribes, including American Indians, poisoned watercourses with toxic plants. We assume that coastal dwellers picked up fish that had been marooned by falling tides. Like farm kids of centuries later, early man probably muddied small ponds and creeks and gathered gasping fish from the surface.

Some of the simple ways of the early fishermen are still highly effective. I have watched a Yucatan native using a plain, round push-

Yucatan fisherman throws a long handline, mixing
an ancient method with modern equipment.

pole to kill gray snappers, often credited as the most intelligent sport fish of all. The man simply shoved his boat against shoreline mangroves and moved slowly along them. When he sighted a fish among the roots he would stab downward with his blunt pole—not even a spear.

Some have guessed that the fishing pole (rod) came from the spear; others believe it developed from the need to get a bait past brush or shallows. It is more likely that these things developed together, one preceding the other in certain parts of the world and the reverse true elsewhere. Development of hooks and lures is easier to follow.

The first lines were probably vines or plant fibers, but time is not kind to such vegetable matter and they have disappeared along with their uses. Hooks are different. The hook seemed to develop from the gorge, and probably fish were first allowed to swallow a large bait attached to a line, then pulled in with nothing else to hold them. That's still done.

The gorge probably began as a simple crosspiece, possibly sharpened on the ends and fastened to the line near its center. The fish could swallow it lengthwise; then when the line came taut the ends of a gorge would pierce the walls of the fish's stomach, or at least catch somewhere in its throat or gills. Fasten the line past center and it begins to become a hook. Ancient men probably saw the possibilities immediately.

There is argument as to whether the hook came directly from the gorge or if the two were developed simultaneously. It's unimportant, but the hooks, especially the modern ones, are a more advanced tool. Hooks were made from naturally forked sticks, from bird beaks, claws, thorns, insect legs, bones, shells and stones. Wood was burned to harden it.

Probably the most complex yet practical hooks were the ornate halibut hooks of the Alaskan Indians, sometimes highly ornamented and with mythological themes. They are prized in modern museums. To take the place of hooks were various materials such as silk fibers or hairs for entangling fish. In the 1980s some modern lures were designed with Velcro instead of hooks, the material (often used to close pockets) intended to snag in a fish's small teeth (such as the black bass's). So that scheme has stood the test of a few thousand years.

Modern spoons, plugs and flies are generally listed separately, but baits of those sorts came early in the game. No one knows how long islanders of the Pacific have used shells as wobbling spoons—and some modern spoons have been made to imitate their iridescent coloring.

There are interesting stories about the modern plug or artificial minnow, but history indicates that it probably appeared first as a decoy. Indians and Eskimos fished through holes in the ice, using spears with decoys (teasers?) to attract fish. The "dark hut" was erected over a hole in the ice to give the fisherman a good view through his opening, and light-colored pebbles were strewn on the bottom to better outline the fish.

A lonely vigil of survival over such ice holes, whether the quarry was fish or seal, is one of the most terrible ordeals of primitive man, less dramatic than confronting a polar bear but a test of stoicism. The watchers sometimes lost their minds while waiting for food that meant life itself. In fact, anyone studying primitive angling regards the Eskimo with awe, for no people have lived in a more hostile environment. The Eskimo has been one of the world's most efficient inventors and a true mechanic with minimal resources.

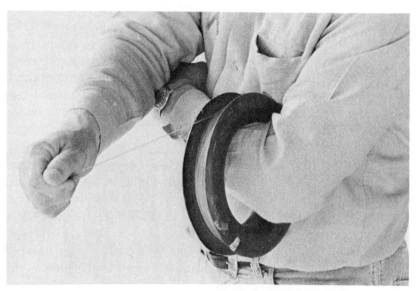

Simplest of all reels is a wooden spool still used
by many handliners.

The jig may have come from the decoy too, but it was used by some of the first professional deep-water fishermen in the traditional up-and-down handline motion. It was used in other ways with modern tackle when it became "modern." Certainly its inventor will never be known.

The feathered fly just possibly might have begun as a sportsman's tool but no one can be sure. Fly fishermen being what they are—generally feeling just a little exclusive—they tend to link any mention of flies directly to people like Charles Cotton of England or Theodore Gordon of the Catskills.

Anyway, the Macedonians of about 200 A.D. (according to Claudius Aelian) were using 6-foot rods and making a fly of wool and rooster neck feathers. Hans Jorgen Hurum in *A History of the Fish Hook* describes a picture of an angler from Thebes (around 1400 B.C.) which involves a butterfly-like insect, inferring fly fishing at that early date. But flies don't necessarily mean sportier fishing. Even today there are instances in which flies would probably take more fish in a short time than any other rod method, a good example being an over-crowded brook trout creek. The artificial fly is not necessarily a sporting gesture, even though it usually is.

There was an ego-crushing salutation of a Colorado resort owner of 30 years ago.

"Fishing is so good now," he said, "that you won't have to use those flies. The trout will bite on worms!"

However, it seems that fly fishing was well advanced by sport fishermen before they had gone far with other artificial lures. Part of this is because the early gentlemen fishermen were largely concerned with trout, and trout have been responsible for fly fishing's lasting popularity.

At the moment we're trying to deal strictly with the beginnings. We cannot find them for poles or rods, though the Egyptians used rods about 2000 B.C. While we have smugly announced stages of reel development in England and France, drawings indicate the Chinese had reels a very long time ago. There is a good 12th century Chinese painting showing a reel in use. Perhaps the important thing is the *purpose* of the reel, and certainly for hundreds of years it was used only for the storage of line and playing fish. It was not used in casting as was the baitcasting reel developed much later.

Although there were ancient fly rods long before Dame Juliana is supposed to have written of them in the *Boke Of St. Albans* (printed in 1496), it is doubtful whether they were used in casting in the sense that the modern fly rod is—a combination of rod thrust and line weight. They were long, and it is probable that they simply dangled the line or flopped it forward with little rod action.

Izaak Walton's *The Compleat Angler* came along in 1653 and the rod seems to have been used much in the "old" way at that time. America's fly fishing was a product of the English methods, though the very long rods were retained longer in Britain. Evidently we can forget true fly casting of the modern type until at least the 18th century, and true baitcasting (turning spool) until well into the nineteenth.

Let's look at America's fish as they were when the first Europeans arrived. Changes since then have been largely our doing, both additions and subtractions, and the remodeling has been almost complete.

The Atlantic salmon no longer makes much impression as a gamefish in the United States, simply because its numbers are few and the sport is expensive. It is important though as it demonstrates the rise and fall of a kind of fishing, and the fierce efforts at renewal which so often follow a fading sport. The revival methods are available although they are very expensive and the salmon's supporters are limited because so exclusive a fish is not exactly democratic in its appeal. Public funds, voters often feel, should be spent on "everybody's" sport.

The salmon is a cold-water fish by definition, but when Columbus arrived there were Atlantic salmon along the coast of what are now the southern states. To the early colonists it was certainly no king of gamefishes. There were too many, and great plenty detracts from any fish's stature.

Coastal streams were so choked by salmon headed upstream to spawn that they could be gathered with pitchforks or nets and hauled away in wagons. They were fed to employees so frequently that some workers' contracts stated a limit on the number of salmon meals that could be served. The fish made good fertilizer and reports are that they were fed to livestock. No species that plentiful could be highly prized as a gamefish.

But when salmon got scarcer they became true prizes for fly fishermen in America as they had been for a long time in Europe, especially in Great Britain. On the European coast they ran as far south as Spain.

There weren't many American sport fishermen in colonial days for two reasons. First, the business of making a home in the wilds, sometimes among hostile Indians, tended to reduce fishing for fun to a trivial thing. Second, the Puritans frowned upon such worldly activities as throwing feathers at fish. Other groups had similarly strict views.

Anyway, even though some salmon were used for fertilizer, the colonists couldn't have depleted the salmon supply if it hadn't been for the industrial practices that polluted the streams. Shipping, logging and manufacturing were important in that. By about 1850 many of the great salmon rivers no longer had any run at all. The fish hung on in Maine for a long time, finally all but disappearing there too. By 1980 the fight to return them to their former routes was showing results, although the yearly ups and downs were discouraging. Always there was a hazard of uncontrolled commercial fishing at sea.

In the 1960s and 1970s when several organizations were fighting to restore U.S. salmon runs (only the Canadian rivers had enough fish to bother with for a long time) the toughest problems were a long way from American shores. For some time it had been known that many of the salmon that spawned in American creeks congregated off northern Europe during much of their ocean existence. European commercial operators caught them there—too many of them.

Hard-nosed diplomacy produced some alleviation of the problem, but salmon lovers still worked under a handicap. Even if the streams were purified, little was gained if the fish never came back. The salmon is a capsule of monumental conservation problems.

Fleets of fishing boats spent the summers off Newfoundland at the cod and haddock banks during much of the time that colonists were scratching for a hold on the eastern seaboard. Those fishermen came from France, Spain, Portugal and England, occasionally guarded by warships when European politics festered. Theirs was a separate world from that of the settlers a little farther south. It seems likely that European fishermen were working the banks before Columbus sailed, probably neither knowing nor caring that they were on the edge of a "New World." There are good indications because the Indians were using words that sounded tantilizingly Basque when John Cabot landed in Newfoundland in 1497.

The terrible hardships of European cod fishermen off the Newfoundland coast were surpassed only by those of actual war. Casualties were high from disease, injury and drowning. There were fishing villages along the northern coast the entire time that settlements were being made farther south, but because they had no political signifi- cance there is little record of them. The more we probe such things the more we realize what slender threads of history have been traced through the ages. It is unusual that we know as much as we do about early fishing.

Second to the Atlantic salmon in prestige for early sport fishermen were the trouts, and America's were very different from the European brown. The Eastern streams had plentiful fish but they were brook trout, generally accepted as easy marks in the wild state. The first English anglers who fished for them considered the brookie (actually a char) too simple-minded to be a true challenge.

The brook trout requires cold, clean water and was unable to com- pete well with the early industrialization of the East. Its habitat was from Labrador to Georgia's mountain streams and west to Hudson Bay, Minnesota and Iowa.

Professional saltwater fishing was vital in colonial days and many of the newcomers counted on fishing as their major occupation. About as close as we can get to saltwater sport fishing of that day is the trolling for bluefish by sailboat and handline, a sort of family picnic affair quite prevalent off Long Island and many other locations.

Shad were plentiful in the eastern rivers at spawning time, and found as far south as Florida. Historians tell of the great plenty of coastal species such as weakfish, striped bass and the mackerels, but these reports are rather general and the supply was subject to great fluctuations, even then. It takes only one bumper crop to produce an impression of constant plenty when no running account is main- tained.

Certainly there was no indication that the black bass would ever be the most popular and most widely distributed of American gamefish. There were none in Europe and no one looked for them in America. The original range of the largemouth was through the Mississippi Valley and along the Atlantic coast south of Maryland and in south- eastern Canada and the Great Lakes region. The smallmouth range is said to have been the St. Lawrence, upper Mississippi, Tennessee and Ohio River drainages and the Great Lakes. These areas are approxi- mate since the basses were almost ignored for more than 200 years,

*Going back to basics, this lady catches a haddock
from a Newfoundland charter boat.
Similar handlines were used there hundreds of years ago.*

then scattered over all of the contiguous states. It seems strange that so prolific a fish hadn't spread its range before getting help from railroads.

In the U.S., the northern pike was found as far south as the Hudson River, the Great Lakes, the Ohio Valley, Missouri and eastern Nebraska. Since it was a resident also of northern Europe and Asia, the first settlers brought its reputation with them and it received more attention than the black bass. The pike not only has an evil appearance but has feeding habits that automatically make it a villain of nature and a logical subject for the most fanciful superstitions. When a freshwater monster was conjured up by some imaginative soul it was generally in the form of a pike. When a primitive taxidermist built a fake monster he often used parts of a pike to add authenticity.

It was said the pike hatched from pieces of waterweed. It would eat or try to eat almost anything that moved, actually an important quality, for a fish that is easy to catch is invaluable as survival food for starving frontiersmen. Anyway, all sorts of diabolical means were worked out by early anglers to capture monster pike. Anything was fair for a fish that ate goslings and caught its prey by ambush.

Taxonomists apparently either ignored the muskellunge or never bothered to publicize their findings, for well into the 20th century there were arguments in sporting magazines as to whether the muskellunge was really a separate fish or just a pike with unusual markings.

Here we have one of the oddities of the angler's nature. The muskie, very scarce and now known to be a somewhat different fish, is the subject of lifetime searches, while the very similar northern pike is scornfully called a "snake" or "jack." *Jack,* incidentally, has become a catchall name for species not considered especially desirable. Literally dozens of fishes are called "jacks."

The muskellunge was a native of the St. Lawrence and Great Lakes areas and was found in the Tennessee system, the Ohio River Basin and in Minnesota and Wisconsin, where it has gained its greatest fame. The smaller Eastern chain pickerel, another look-alike of the northern pike, is found in the South as well as in northern pike range. Of course it too is called a jack in many places. The northern pike has been scattered widely in northern waters of the U.S. and Canada and muskellunge range has also been extended.

The rainbow trout was native only west of the Rockies, and the steelhead is simply a famous seagoing version which gets larger than creek and river dwellers, although it's often surpassed by landlocked rainbows in some Western lakes. It was almost 300 years before the European arrivals learned much about the rainbow. Of course early visitors to California were exposed to it, but little was reported at the time.

On both sides of the Continental Divide were many species of cutthroat trout, primarily considered an inland fish but having some seagoing representatives. Fishermen visiting some of the fine streams of the West, also containing rainbows, browns and brook trout, are sometimes surprised to learn that the cutthroat was originally the only trout there. Cutthroat strains are difficult to follow, for the tribes mix genetically and even hybridize freely with the rainbow.

Some of the strangely colored trout of isolated areas owe their hue to their surroundings and are prone to be assimilated by other strains. Color, considered highly important by the casual observer, is a very unreliable guide for the serious biologist.

The grayling has fallen upon hard times in much of its early range. The Michigan grayling has disappeared, demanding even higher water quality than the brook trout, which followed it in some waters only to be replaced by more adaptable rainbow and brown trout as habitat was degraded by civilization. There are a few grayling in Montana and Wyoming today and many in Canada and Alaska. Like trout, the grayling was in demand by early sport fishermen since it is a well-known fish in Europe.

The Pacific salmon, five of them, spawn in fresh water, go to sea and then return to spawn once and die. This is unique, for although most other salmonids have saltwater representatives, they are capable of spawning more than once. Pacific salmon are a successful introduction to the Great Lakes, but they do not reproduce naturally there, that population being maintained by artificial spawning.

The Dolly Varden trout is a char very similar to the arctic char. Not especially prized for food it is called "bull trout." Some of them are anadromous. The arctic char is quite plentiful about the Far North for those making the long trip, and is easily caught on sporting tackle during its migrations.

The lake trout, Mackinaw, or togue is a char that reaches great size and was at one time the mainstay of the Great Lakes fishery. Probably few casual pioneer fishermen caught lake trout except for brief periods in the northern part of their range. They are mainly residents of the depths, sometimes hundreds of feet down, in cold, clear lakes with a minimum of fertility where the fish population is extremely limited. Their presence at great depth adds mystery and glamour for freshwater anglers—a fish hardly ever seen until hooked.

The original haunts of the laker were in the Northeast and scattered across Canada and Alaska, but just where the fish was native and where it has been introduced is largely a mystery.

In addition to these best-known fish there are a number of smaller relatives in fresh water and a great many in salt water that sport fishermen did not even consider until almost 1900. The truth is that tackle required some advancement before some of the best gamefish could be hooked. The Pilgrims couldn't have handled a swordfish.

The few American sport fishermen kept looking back to Britain for instruction. It took a revolution and some tackle developments of their own before American sportsmen began to make their marks. And with good and poor judgment and endless enthusiasm, Americans moved their gamefish about like careless chess players.

CHAPTER THREE

FIRST SPORT FISHERMEN

It would be easy to get carried away and turn this whole thing into a study of old fishing classics. When dealing with the earliest sport fishing, it's equally easy to become a literary critic—an ego trip we can't afford. Let's try to stay fairly close to the facts.

Anything we know about early sport fishing was written by people who may have been authors first and fishermen second. Thus our most famous fishermen were not necessarily the best or most informed anglers of their time, but simply the most literarily inclined.

To some extent this carries over to the present when the best known anglers are those who write about it or appear in fishing television shows. Some of the very best anglers are completely unknown and have never written a word about their skills or achievements. We have to live with this situation and make the most of it. Let's briefly check the backgrounds of some of the best-known writers that have furnished our information.

We can designate Izaak Walton (probably not the correct way of spelling his first name, but the way it got started on the first edition of

The Compleat Angler) as a patron saint of anglers, his name having become so synonymous with sport fishing that it is used by people who haven't the slightest idea of his status as an angler.

There is much evidence that Walton lifted many of the ideas for his treasured work from earlier writers, and if he did no more than put them together in one place, we can still use his name. But there is more to it than that, for the work of Walton is truly classical as the almost endless editions of it can testify.

Izaak Walton was a London ironmonger, not of nobility, but highly educated and a friend of literary people. In the sometimes violent politics of the day he was a Royalist, although I understand most of the businessmen were on the Parliament side. Walton's writing was so charming a portrayal of the angler's philosophy that it is a shame to cast any shadow of literary thievery, but in 1954 a single copy of a book titled *The Art of Angling* surfaced, and with it the evidence that Walton's work was not completely original in theme.

Walton's first edition is dated at 1653 and *The Art of Angling,* author uncertain, was published in 1577. The earlier book uses a device of dialogue between two men, Viator and Piscator, the same two fishermen quoted by Walton as the basis for his book. Piscator is the expert, Viator the student. The Walton book also contains a great deal of the same material found in *The Art of Angling.* Although the similarity of presentation is too obvious to be accidental, the Walton artistry is distinctive. To anyone reading for pleasure, the original sources of the ideas are academic.

Long before Walton there was a much hazier personality, Dame Juliana Berners, who is said to have been the abbess of a convent and who had written some material on hunting. Then when we find the *Treatyse of Fisshynge Wyth an Angle* in *The Boke of St. Albans* (1496), it's a little surprising to see that she is *automatically* credited with it, evidently because she did a hunting section in an earlier edition. The fishing material is extremely practical, especially in description of flies.

It is questioned whether Dame Berners wrote it, whether that's the correct spelling of her name, and whether there ever was such a person. But we don't know what else to call the "Dame Juliana flies" and I doubt if we will ever know any more about the author of the *Treatyse* than we do now. I think it is nice to have Dame Juliana in fishing history, whether she was real or not.

John McDonald, in *Quill Gordon,* did a careful study on Dame Juliana and finished with this masterpiece:

"We have plausibly proved, we think, that as author of *The Treatise of Fishing With an Angle,* Dame Juliana is a myth. But in elevating our recognition of her from legend to true myth, we have provided anglers with what they really want."

There is hardly anybody today who actually believes in the physical existence of Diana, goddess of the hunt, as she appears in Greek mythology, but it is not unusual to have her figure engraved on a modern presentation shotgun. She looks pretty (at least the way the engravers do her) and she means *hunting,* so why not? Anyway, Dame Juliana is all right with me.

We should introduce one other authority before we get on with the fishing facts. That's Charles Cotton, who wrote part of the later editions of *The Compleat Angler* and was a much younger associate of Walton. Walton, although seemingly a master at bait fishing, was no fly fishing expert, and Cotton was. Cotton was a very different personality, born to the aristocracy. He produced considerable literature, both prose and poetry. Some of it was considered pretty earthy for its time and later critics seemed to tolerate Cotton's presence only because he had the fly fishing stuff in his department.

We'll quote from numerous other British authorities of Walton's time and a little later but we'll treat their backgrounds, if necessary, as we come to their contributions. Let's look at just a few of the nuts and bolts of angling before Dame Juliana's time.

Most of the very old accounts of fishing list bait mixtures that would put the most odoriferous of modern catfish concoctions to shame. There's an inclination to read some of the recipes twice to see if they really do include quantities of human blood or flesh. It's hard to believe it the first time through. Some of the methods of securing the best of maggots and other worms must have required strong stomachs. Deceased and well-ripened cats were prized.

Through most of the early writings runs a familiar theme of how the fishing waters had been reduced and the number of fishermen had been increased until the good old days seemed to be gone forever. So 20th century sportsmen feeling put upon by over-pressured water can at least find kindred feelings in the anglers of hundreds of years ago.

From the first, there have been admonitions to fishermen to close

"Trout Fishing at Wagon Wheel Gap," Colorado, in the 1890s.
(Photo courtesy of The Museum of American Fly Fishing, Inc.)

gates, take care of private property and release undersized fish. The subject of poaching on private property isn't treated extensively. Poaching has been a way of life in some European circles and not considered too much of a disgrace.

Clear through the time of Walton there was not much distinction between rough fish and gamefish. The salmon was considered a prize but the trouts and grayling were generally considered equal with the roach, a carp-like fish considered a "rough" fish today. This attitude is in keeping with the feeling that fishing method was not a matter of status. Fly fishing had been practiced for some time when Walton appeared, but it had been generally considered just another way to fish, to be used when the fish were taking flies, but no more prestigious than worm fishing. The fly fishing cult was beginning to appear about the time of Walton and Cotton and for centuries has produced controversy as to method. It is safe to say that Britain was the mother of "technical" fly fishing.

Charles Chenevix Trench wrote *A History of Angling,* published in 1974, a top-notch work keyed strongly to the British scene. Before discussing Dame Juliana's *Treatise,* Trench cites the oldest English fishing literature as coming from *The Colloquy of Aelfric,* Archbishop of Canterbury, in A.D. 995, but explains that it's impossible to tell whether that writer was fishing for sport or professionally. He also points to fishing in Japan, going back to somewhere around A.D. 200 with Japanese royalty. Japanese interest in angling came down through the centuries, the aristocracy maintaining fishing pavilions for angling in comfort. Japan had a god of angling, Ebisu. Trench also cites brief Flemish angling material and a Latin work of 1480 showing a fisherman using a float.

The *Treatise* tells us a great deal of fishing equipment and method. Let's look at the recommended rod.

You might be surprised that it was in three pieces and used for both bait and fly fishing. It was 13 to 14 feet long, the top section of hazel, the middle section of willow, ash or hazel, and the butt of blackthorn, crab or medlar. There's no mention of a reel and illustrations of fishermen of that time in England don't show them. We know they were in use in China and probably elsewhere.

That rod was jointed by a burned socket in the larger section with the smaller section seated in it. The hooks were made from needles with efficient bending, heating and tempering. The leader (although it wasn't called that) was made of horsehair, the number of strands depending upon the size of fish to be caught. The line was a little longer than the rod. Horsehair was to have a long tenure as line and leader.

Although the art was well-advanced by then, the *Treatise* indicates most of the tackle was made by the fisherman and gives practical instruction in that. The horsehair lines were made by twisting operations with a variety of tools and were tapered by sections. Although this gave fine tippets that were satisfactorily strong (check some horsehair yourself), the lines were not likely to slip easily through rod guides. In fact, guides apparently weren't in any common use.

The long rods were well-adapted to a "dibbling" form of fly fishing and were good for precise placement of delicate natural baits. European fishermen have consistently used long rods or poles for much of the fishing that Americans do by true casting, and the casting has been a great part of the game for Americans. Now and then there is a reversion to the old methods which comes on as a new development. A notable example was in modern bass tournament fishing in the 1970s, and that appeared as "flipping," popular in California. It is simply use of a long rod to apply a lure to a very small opening in vegetation. No real casting can be quite so accurate and in selected waters the "flippers" were money winners, using long rods with spinning reels.

With the long rod that is not used in a brisk casting motion, the most fragile of natural baits can be lowered with a minimum of violence. The only special hazard is that the rod tip will be highly visible to the fish. However, one bass fishing method in America ("jiggerbobbing" or "doodlesocking") keeps a surface lure moving so violently that the rod tip is hidden by turbulence. At any rate, the angler of Juliana's day was not greatly handicapped on the smaller streams. There is no indication that the tapered horsehair line was ever heavy enough to bring out what is called "rod action" in modern fly fishing. The *Treatise* has detailed instructions for dyeing horsehair with different tints for different seasons. Later users of it generally strove for a neutral color.

Juliana described all sorts of baits, natural and mixed, and the concoctions she explains are relatively simple, none of them requiring grave robbing or manslaughter. She goes into detail in instructing the angler to keep out of sight of the fish, a matter that made considerable impression on historians who point out so modern an approach. But it's logical that hiding from the fish was very nearly the first requirement for any fisherman, whether he used a 14-foot pole or a club.

The instruction goes all the way from minnows to salmon and pike, and one phase of pike fishing is especially intriguing for anyone who wants an extra thrill. If you wanted to spice the action once the pike was hooked, she said, "then tie the cord to a goose's foot; and you shall see good hauling, whether the goose or the pike shall have the better."

It is assumed that the unfortunate goose was used for trolling, a sort of extension of the cast on broader waters.

The Juliana handmade hooks (from square-headed needles) did not have eyes, but the upper part of the shank was broadened to hold horsehair for snelling and the thread that helped to secure it, fastened by wrapping and whipping. Use of the eyed hook was not common in early angling, even though it must have been no novelty.

The thing about Juliana's work that appeals most to modern fishermen is her listing and description of a dozen flies for trout, salmon and grayling, and she lists them as if they were no novelty but had been used for a long time. British writers consider most of them imitation flies rather than impression or "fancy" flies, but in some cases they do not agree as to just what insect the flies imitate.

The materials for the flies were simple. The bodies were made of wool of various colors and the wings came from partridge, "red cock," drake and buzzard. This does not mean that in the proper sizes the flies did not mimic May flies, stone flies and caddis flies. In fact, some were close enough to modern ties that many of their describers routinely tagged them with modern names. They would, of course, catch fish today. She listed them by the months of appropriate natural insect hatches.

Juliana's work came along at about the same time as the printing process. Lack of it had undoubtedly doomed earlier works to extinction.

Walton's book has become the classic of a contemplative life along the stream. Many read it over and over in the various editions, not to learn fishing tactics but to assimilate a poetically presented philosophy. Walton was no backpacking pioneer of virgin trout streams, but a lover of the civilized countryside.

But with all of his concoctions of natural baits and careful approaches to the fish, there is one special bit of information by Walton that catches the eye of Americans. He tells of the artificial minnow, made up 200 years before Jim Heddon whittled his plug. It was like this:

> ". . . made by a handsome woman with a fine hand,
> and a live minnow lying by her; the mould or body of the
> minnow was cloth, and wrought upon, or over it, thus
> with a needle; then the back of it with very sad French green
> silk and paler green silk towards the belly, shadowed as perfectly
> as you can imagine, just as you see a minnow; the belly was
> wrought also with a needle, and it was a part of it white silk, and
> another part of it with silver thread; the tail and fins were of a
> quill which was shaved thin; the eyes were of two little black
> beads, and the head was so shadowed, and all of it so cunningly
> wrought, and so exactly dissembled that it would beguile any
> sharp-sighted trout in a swift stream."

That kind of lure was evidently the forerunner of the Phantom, Devil and Devon minnows—favorites in Britain in various forms long before the American "plug."

Walton was an expert at "spinning" with a natural minnow. The term has been used to mean so many things in fishing that it needs explanation: in his case it involved hooking and working a minnow so that it actually spun when pulled through the water. Such a lure is a line twister if not equipped with swivels, which were used in Walton's time, whether by him or not.

When Charles Cotton wrote his contribution for Walton's work, he listed a great many flies, including those of Dame Juliana. He described in detail the methods of tying flies and didn't mention a vise. He used a collection of materials approaching what more recent operators would have at hand.

Cotton didn't wax quite so philosophical as Walton did, although when appearing in Walton's book he maintained the same format his elder had. One of his bits of advice may possibly be the most quoted of

*Before split bamboo became popular, fly fishermen used
solid wood. Fly fishing is the oldest form of
light-tackle gamefishing.*

any regarding fly fishing for trout, saying: "To fish fine and far off is the first and principal rule for trout angling."

Cotton advocated matching the length of the rod to the size of the river and said 15 to 18 feet long would be enough. Evidently rod building had come a long way by that time. He describes as follows:

> "Of these, the best that ever I saw are made in Yorkshire, which are all of one piece; that is to say, of several, six, eight, ten or twelve pieces, so neatly placed and tied together with fine thread below, and silk above, as to make it taper, like a switch, and to ply with a true bent to your hand; and these too are light, being made of fir wood nearer to the top, that a man might very easily manage the longest of them that ever I saw, with one hand; and these when you have given over angling for a season, being taken to pieces, and laid up in some dry place, may afterwards be set together again in their former postures. . . ."

Incidentally, the matter of reducing rods to short sections had a purpose other than convenience for many early fishermen. Their sport was not universally accepted as a worthwhile pastime and anglers frequently desired to slip through or past the multitude with their purpose unknown. Therefore, many early rods took down so that they could be concealed or could masquerade as walking sticks. The practice continued into America, especially in Puritan neighborhoods. The modern "suitcase" rod is handy but it also has advantages of concealment. The word "poaching" is seldom publicly associated with short rod sections, but many clandestine fishing trips on forbidden waters have started with short rod packages.

With a light, 15-foot rod, a fisherman could, indeed, fish *"fine and far off,"* using a tippet of two horsehairs and a line a little longer than the rod. With such gear you won't compete for distance with a Pacific steelhead fisherman, but you'll get 30 feet if the wind is favorable.

Cotton goes into detail in telling his readers to cast with the wind and doesn't seem to worry much whether the fly goes upstream or downstream. Upstream and downstream fly fishing were two distinctly different methods in the view of somewhat later experts and they argued the relative merits through thousands of pages. However, with the long rod and the short line the methods were fairly interchangeable. So too were wet and dry fly fishing.

Today, most of us are obsessed with true casting, using line weight and rod action to throw the fly, and since that has become part of the fun for us we aren't much interested in sneakily lowering a fly just below our rod tips. Also, we seldom use pure wind casts in which the fly is delivered by the breeze alone, something that works well with a very long rod and light, tapered horsehair line. The long rod was good for allowing a natural fly, captured during a hatch, to be carried out by the wind.

Then there was the business of shortening the line and setting the fly on the trout's nose by lowering it from concealment on the bank. With the short line a fly could be delivered as a dry, even though it wouldn't float for long, then allowed to sink as it was passed downstream and worked back as a wet fly or streamer. They didn't say much about whether the flies floated or not and some indicated it didn't make much difference. Even while facing almost downstream, it is possible to make short floats with a long rod without any complex casting maneuvers. Cotton did say it was sometimes necessary to sink the line on a very windy day to prevent its being blown off the water and taking the fly with it.

Here we are back in the time of Walton and already involved in "impression" and "imitation" flies, and although those authors don't say so we're already into the business of streamers, dry flies, nymphs and wet flies.

Generally, the dry fly, floating high on the surface, is recognized as a freshly-hatched insect, although it may be a terrestrial (land insect that reached the water by accident), or spinner (insect that has died or is about to die after depositing its eggs). The wet fly represents drowned flies, the nymph represents insects not yet matured and living in the water, and the streamer usually represents a small fish.

Of course these are arbitrary definitions, used as a guide, and are more rigidly defined by the fisherman than by the fish. They are a route to fly manipulation so the fisherman at least has in mind what he is *trying* to imitate.

It would seem that the flies Cotton used weren't very high floaters and certainly those of Dame Juliana would tend to watersoak pretty promptly, but with those long rods they could keep the fly on top for part of a "dead drift." Then if it sank and became a "drowned" insect there were no complaints and it could be fished downstream in tradi-

44

tional wet fly or nymph fashion. Let it swing around in the stream and it would serve as a streamer since few nymphs are as swift as a streamer swinging in a brisk current.

It seems that those early anglers had all of the drills and lacked only modern terminology to walk right into a fly fisherman's club and join the discussion. But the true "dry" fly waited for some time for its name, and was "discovered" in various locations at different times.

We may have to guess at some of the qualities of early tackle but it's easy to check on others. For example, many snoopers through angling antiquity have checked the qualities of horsehair lines and leaders. I note that Joe Brooks and his rancher friend Len Kinke concluded that the average good horsehair would test about 2½ pounds and that's about what I found in my clumsy experiments, which resulted in my sneaking out to catch a trout with a single strand. Many modern fishermen, fishing "fine and far off," use monofilament leaders that test less than that. Brooks stated that he had found a few British anglers using horsehair tippets in recent years and that British merchants told him they had sold horsehair lines into the 1930s.

Cotton, who seemed to believe in two strands for his trout fishing, was therefore dealing with something like five-pound-test, enough to handle big fish easily in open water on modern tackle, but remember that he wasn't using a reel. It seems that reels were in occasional use at that time but they were clumsy wooden winches, employed mainly by salmon fishermen. Through all of this it is good to note that Cotton did his fishing on the Dove, a stream of fairly open water and traditional trout dimensions. Walton fished there with him but also in other places.

All of the early commentators explained the use of the rod's bend in playing a fish. Walton said that when the fish was too much to work to shore he would simply toss the rod into the water and let the quarry wear itself out by towing it around. Cotton didn't do that and seems a bit taken aback by his old friend's method, but then landing a big fish with no reel and a 15-foot rod can get awkward unless you have some help.

Evidently Cotton always had some help because he says: ". . . in landing of a fish, which every one that can afford to angle for pleasure, has somebody to do for him. . . ."

There were landing nets in plenty of early illustrations and Cotton could undoubtedly afford a helper on his excursions. Probably Walton could too, but Walton's love for the solitude of the pastoral stream doesn't seem to fit in with an ever-present gillie.

It seems a little strange that small and convenient reels weren't in use then, for technology had certainly gone that far (consider the ornate clocks of the time). But anglers of that time had the inconvenience of splices in horsehair lines. There were "loops" on many rods of the time, allowing considerable line to be carried. Some fishermen wrapped the line on a tool resembling a bobbin. Some simply trailed extra line behind them along the stream or coiled it in their hands. Line baskets or trays have been used off and on for a long time and the French were using them in the 17th century. Some American fishermen carry them today for holding shooting line. Brass multiplying reels were in common use by 1770.

It seems that Walton and Cotton used only one fly to a line, but droppers were in use by other anglers, some of them using so many it seemed somewhat like a trotline on a rod. While horsehair continued most popular as leader material, catgut and silkworm gut were available after 1600. Silkworm had been used for a long time in China. Earlier silkworm gut was simply stretched into long strands after being removed from the worm; the later material was "drawn" by being pulled through small holes in steel plates.

The truly dry fly evidently appeared on the scene gradually through refined tying, better materials and chemical dressings. In 1590 Leonard Mascall suggested making flies with cork bodies, a practice which evidently didn't catch on immediately.

In *The Complete Troller,* Thomas Nobbes (1682) preferred silk line for pike and claimed to cast 20 yards through a ring on his rod tip.

By present standards, fishermen of near Walton's time were not great travelers and their reports obviously cover waters of very limited areas. Cotton seems to write almost entirely about the Dove. However, anglers like Richard Franck, who wrote *Northern Memoirs,* had fished in Scotland for salmon. Robert Venables, whose work appeared in some Walton editions, had pursued salmon in Ireland.

The fishing material of the time really came from a small area geographically—England—and a researcher is bound to have unanswered questions about what was going on in the rest of the world. It simply wasn't recorded.

The angling authors evidently didn't use boats much and most of them fished waters that could be handled from the bank, since it was settled farming country. Evidently there hadn't been much effort at wading equipment by the time Venables wrote: "In small brooks you may angle upwards or else in great rivers you must wade as I have known some who thereby got the sciatica. I would not wish you to pursue pleasure at so dear a rate."

Procedure became so conventional and so traditional that new inventions in method or gear came on very slowly or were rejected entirely. There was little pioneering for new water in so tight a community.

The eventual feeling that trout and salmon were the most aristocratic fish was expressed by William Lawson as early as 1613, when he wrote, "The trout makes the angler the most gentlemanly and readiest sport of all other fishes. If you fish with a made fly, this is the chief pleasure in angling."

It was about 300 years later that such an attitude became familiar in America, where the British traditions were accepted by many, but the much larger company of black bass fishermen with baitcasting and spinning tackle would take exception.

Those would be fighting words to the pilots of thousands of high-speed bassboats with ticking, buzzing and flickering fish-finding instruments and carrying tackle boxes the size of steamer trunks.

CHAPTER FOUR

THE RODS

As plugcasters, spinfishermen and trollers consider the reel their most important piece of equipment, the fly fisherman treasures his rod. So when we get into the history of fishing rods we emphasize fly casting.

In most cases, new materials and techniques of rod building are first tried in fly rods. Rod "action," the basis of all modern fly angling, is such a subtle quality that you'll hear no two rods are alike. This may be technically true although those differences are so infinitesimal in glass, graphite or boron that I don't think any caster can find the variations in different individuals of some models. It's somewhat different in bamboo; I believe the miniscule idiosyncrasies can be felt by a long-experienced caster who has used one rod for several hours and then handles another cane rod that's supposed to be just like it. Tom Morgan of Winston says that each completed cane rod is taken out and cast by the builders and that invariably they will select certain tips as being outstanding, even when others fit their rigid specifications.

Ardent fly fishermen tend to be rod collectors, some of them keeping a picket fence of rods, most of which they never use. The truth is

An old Hardy rod (upper) shows the great number
of wrappings used before glues were perfected.
Modern rod (lower) has wraps only at guides.

that a great deal of learned rod discussion is so much baloney, as are some of the tackle shop tests for rod qualities. And some who own rods built by the old masters could cast just as well or better with inexpensive glass.

Above all though, it must be remembered that there is as much difference between individual fishermen as between individual fishing rods. Fishing rods must be fitted to the fisherman's method, however poetic or crude. Perhaps this is the reason why the products of great bamboo rod builders may all be called perfect, even though they are very different in feel. It is a little strange when the same man calls them all perfect for his purposes, because they can't be.

We must mention these things because rod history invariably becomes partly the history of famous rod builders. It is one part of fishing where the manufacturer becomes the hero.

Before getting into more detail and more precise chronology, let's see how the rods developed, forgetting materials temporarily.

The first ones were simply poles to get the bait or lure farther out. Some historians think they came from spears and others disagree. No matter. Early rods grew in length through the years and were up to 14 or more feet long by the time sport angling began to be recorded. They were made in sections very early in the game, spliced by cords or "jointed" ferrules, the same rod often made of several materials.

When reels came along they were fastened far enough from the butt for one hand above and one below, whether the rod was used for flies or bait. The pole was generally too heavy for one hand, anyway. The two-handed salmon rod, still used by a few anglers, mainly Europeans on both sides of the channel, retains the old reel location. It was popular in America until about 1945. The one-handed rod for light fly fishing became popular during the 19th century, simply because materials and action were developed for it; bamboo was an important contributing factor. It was nearly 100 years before lighter materials such as glass produced fly rods to be used with one hand and intended for throwing heavy lines and bulky lures to 100-pound fish. That came with new casting techniques and more efficient lines.

The baitcasting or plugcasting rod and its cousin, the spinning rod, got a slower start. Clear up until the late 19th century, "casting" rods (used for live and cut bait) were quite long. Even the Henshall bait rod for bass, billed as a breakthrough for convenience, was about 8 feet.

The Rods

The modern freshwater baitcasting rod of 5 or 6 feet came along much later, together with new casting techniques that used rod action in a different way. While the other rods got shorter, the surf rod developed in the other direction and produced awesome distances over what Frank Woolner called the "high surf."

Saltwater trolling rods went from a variety of woods to split cane and to glass and graphite, carefully attuned to the line strengths intended for them.

When graphite lightened fly rods, there was a trend toward longer ones, some nearly as long as rods of a century before, but light enough for convenient one-hand operation. With the development of split bamboo, the fly reel had moved gradually below the rod handle sometime in the 1800s. With the advent of the level-wind, lighter baitcasting rods had even appeared without a foregrip. Spinning rod designers had a hard time figuring where to fasten their reels.

Strangely, after all of the new materials, including steel, glass, graphite and boron, many fishermen show preference for flyrods made 100 years ago. I suspect such preferences are largely based on tradition rather than efficiency. So far, I find the newer rods usually are better rods, even better than bamboo. Of course there are exceptions.

We have to go back to Dame Juliana again so we might as well do it now.

As said before, we're not sure there was a Dame Juliana, but whoever wrote the *Treatise* went into detail on the construction of fishing rods. You have to guess that only a small percentage of the fishermen of the time actually had carefully made poles. It is pretty obvious that a sapling cut at the scene of action would serve well, but there's no doubt Juliana's recommended rod would be handier and could have a somewhat controlled action.

The instruction was to cut a smooth 6-foot (or longer if you wished) section of hazel, willow or aspen between September and February, to be heated in a baking oven and then straightened. It was to be dried for four weeks or more on "exactly squared timber," tied to a bench and made hollow all the way through with a heated wire and burned into an interior taper that would accept the tip of the 2-piece rod. Then the butt section would be waxed, unfastened from the bench and dried "in a smokehouse or up under the house roof."

Then came another section of white hazel to be dried and straightened and bound together with the tip of the rod, which was made from a shoot of blackthorn, crabtree, medlar or juniper. Then the two smaller sections would be fitted into the hollow butt and the butt tapered. Metal ferrules would strengthen the ends of the resulting staff. The tip would be strengthened with a horsehair wrap and a cord loop would be permanently attached to it for fastening the line. No reel was involved.

By the time Joseph Cotton did his writing with Walton about 1676, merchants were specializing in fishing equipment. Here were rods long enough to get considerable distance, even without shooting line. Cotton says, " . . . and for a trout river, one of five or six yards long is commonly enough, and longer (though ever so neatly and artificially made) it ought not to be, if you intend to fish at ease, and if otherwise, where lies the sport?"

Let's see what a 15-footer will do if simply flopping the line. The best canepole fishermen I have watched generally use a line about two feet longer than their poles and manage to get the whole works straight out as they "cast." Fifteen feet isn't especially long for a canepole. This gives more than 30 feet of coverage, and many a fly-fishing trout angler spends a whole day without casting farther than

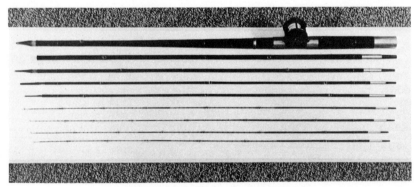

The oldest fly rod in the collection of
The Museum of American Fly Fishing was built in 1832,
possibly in New York. It was a five-piece, twelve-foot,
solid wood rod. Notice that there are four tips and two
fourth sections. The maker is unknown.
(Photo courtesy of The Museum of American Fly Fishing, Inc.)

that. For that matter, some expert panfishermen use short sections of modern fly line on their light canepoles.

Most canepolers simply swing the bait underhanded if it's heavy, and throw it overhanded if it's light. In the overhanded swing they use more rod action than most of them realize. Although the use of long rods remained more popular in mainland Europe and England than in America, a large share of America's casual fishermen still use canepoles of up to 20 feet long.

Until about 1950 there were a great many long canepoles sold in sections with ferrules, some of them with guides and quite a few with handles wrapped with wicker or molded to look like it. Inexpensive glass spincasting rods with pushbutton reels finally pushed the sectioned canepole into the background, although it is still around. A refinement is the fiberglass telescoping pole. Anyway, Cotton and Walton weren't impoverished as to usable equipment.

The model of Cotton's is more rod than pole. Early drawings show fishermen using rods with one hand, but when there was no reel I see little point in that until the second hand was needed for landing a fish.

The takedown feature that conceals the upper sections inside the butt was a convenience for transportation, the whole thing serving as

Old hickory fly rod, probably made before 1850.
(Photo by Warren Shepard)

a walking staff of sorts, but in those days a concealed rod was handy.

Evidently there were no tackle dealers at all in Juliana's time and the fishermen made their own equipment. Anyway, it was a great deal of work to build her described rod. Its weight and flexibility depended upon the options and skills of the maker. It was undoubtedly a relief to well-to-do anglers to be able to buy ready-made rods.

Some of the earlier rod materials lasted in solid form through split bamboo and steel. Greenheart, for example, was available from some tackle dealers up until 1930.

A very large share of the rods used up until the late 1800s were made up of more than one kind of wood. Whalebone, certainly tough and flexible, was used for many tips; that too held on for a long time after better materials were available. Following World War II, there were some short whalebone casting rods made in Japan. They worked with baitcasting or spinning reels but lacked worthwhile action.

The list of woods used in fishing rods is ridiculously long and without the Latin designations it's hard to tell just what some of the exotics were. At risk of offending a student of the subject, I can list these as the best known: bethabara, snakewood, dagama, serviceberry, lancewood, greenheart, mahoe, ash, maple, hickory, Osage orange, basswood, ironwood, hornbeam, cedar, barberry, Calcutta bamboo and Tonkin cane. I parrot these names from early writers and can't tell most of them apart. Greenheart is the best known of the solid woods used prior to split bamboo. English makers had access to a wide variety of woods because of Britain's worldwide commerce.

Henshall said second-growth, close-grained white ash was best for rod butts, calling it "straight-grained, light, springy and strong." He preferred lancewood for second sections and tips, but thought it too heavy for butt sections. He thought greenheart was next to lancewood for tips, but that it was pretty heavy for entire rods or lower sections.

In Henshall's time, Calcutta bamboo was considered best of all. Tonkin cane hadn't come into its own—or rather, across the Pacific, in important quantities. He explained that native American canes are lighter, although not so strong and durable as Chinese or Japanese cane. He thought cedar made a fine rod but that it was not tough enough or strong enough for the "ordinary angler."

When the sport fishing show really got going in America late in the

19th century, sporting goods dealers attached seductive names to various woods and advertised them in hyperbolic language. The old catalogs are stuffed with extravagant claims of strength and resilience, most of which had little or nothing to do with the fishing qualities of the product.

The beginning of split bamboo rods is the most important event of rod development to most students. Up until then, it seems, we hadn't done much better than Walton and Cotton.

When it came to "rent and glue" rods, a craftsman had a chance to express himself. He had control over the medium and could inject the rod with a "personality" so worshiped by bamboo lovers.

Lamination of strips of cane had been done for rod tips long before anyone made an entire rod that way. The conventional bamboo rod of today is almost invariably made of six strips. The first "section bamboo" seems to have surfaced in England around 1800, but it was much later that the "ideal" of six strips was reached. Apparently there were four strips used as early as 1801, with ash or hickory butts. Several British makers had such rods on display during the 1840s. The first laminations probably resulted from the many faults in solid cane as it arrived from Asia.

Whatever contributions were made by earlier builders, Samuel Phillippe of Easton, Pennsylvania, is generally credited as the first builder of a complete flyrod of six strips of bamboo. When it's discussed by succeeding generations, we get the impression that it was a dramatic breakthrough. It might have been, but not everyone thought that the use of six strips was the final answer. Four-strip rods were built 100 years after Phillippe's rod of about 1845 or 1846. Most famous of the 4-strip rods was the Edwards *Quadrate*. Many are still in use.

Phillippe was primarily a gunsmith and apparently had no thought of making it big with fishing gear. He also made violins. His son, Solon, built a complete 6-stripper by 1859. He said his father had made them earlier, but minor disagreement exists as to the exact dates.

With the dawn of split bamboo, we must elaborate a little on what glamorizes it and why its worshipers are among the most fanatical students of fishing equipment. The whole process of construction is subject to so many controls and variables that the great rod builders

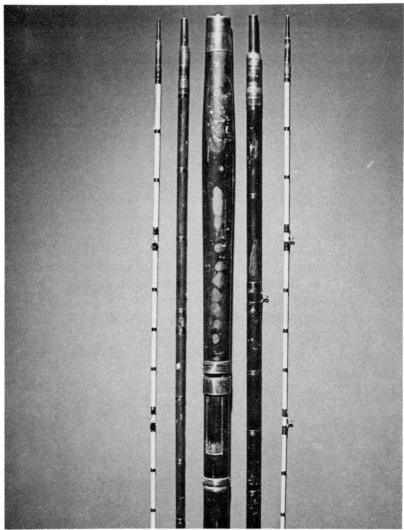

The oldest salmon rod in the collection of
The Museum of American Fly Fishing was in use in 1852.
The rod was a 16-foot, four-piece solid wood rod with two tips.
Its guides were replaced at some time with modern snake guides.
There is a small plaque mounted high on the butt section that
reads, "God Bout River, 21 lbs, July 6th, 1852."
The God Bout is a well known Canadian salmon river.
(Photo courtesy of The Museum of American Fly Fishing, Inc.)

are revered as are the old masters in any other art—even though their disciples are rather limited in number.

In the beginning, it takes the proper cane. For many years after bamboo came into use it was believed that the best was produced in India. "Calcutta" was the magic name for it. Then came the Tonkin cane grown in a rather small area of China under specific climatic conditions.

Rod quality and performance depend partly upon selection of the individual stalk or "culm" of cane; the mystic factors involve density and age. Once selected, the culm is split and shaped by planing in tapered forms, precise grooves in wood or metal. Steel is preferred by modern makers. Judgment is required in straightening, which involves careful heat application. Applied heat can also greatly affect action. A few of the highly superior casting rods have been "burned brittle." Generally, these super-casters are more inclined to breakage.

The "nodes," or raised rings, around the stalk must be dealt with and early makers handled this in several ways. Before being glued, the strips must be adjusted to keep the node areas from appearing side by side or opposite each other and thus weakening the shaft.

The cane of later rods is pieced together so that the tough outside of the original stalk is on the exterior for maximum strength, the result of considerable experimentation with other designs. Gluing was especially difficult in early construction, for the animal glues lacked the waterproof qualities of later mixtures that appeared after World War I.

In more recent rods, there is little thread wrapping except at ferrules and guides. A few early rods were actually wrapped solid with silk thread, the thread being essential as an aid to the glue. Later, the glue was as strong as the cane itself. In a few cases the quality of a rod was indicated by the number of silk wrappings. Then when the glue really held it became obvious that thread would alter the action for better or worse.

The fine tolerances involved are seldom realized. The cane is cut to thousandths of an inch, precision generally reserved for metals. Through the years makers have been very conscious of the effects of miniscule variations in outside measurements. John James Hardy was quoted in 1906:

"One sixty-fourth part of an inch more or less in the butt of an 18-foot rod will make or mar that rod."

Early fly rods, especially those made of solid wood, were gradually tapered at the handles. This "pool cue" silhouette was used in early split-bamboo rods, but a distinct handle, separated from the working part of the rod, became customary within a few years. Various attractive woods formed early handles, and then came cork—generally in a ring shape on the more expensive models and wrapped on in thin sheets for cheaper ones. Some of the finest rods used very narrow rings, possibly as an indication that time was unimportant in building so fine an instrument. That was very nearly true.

For many years there was a procession of patent applications for various types of ferrules. Earlier solid-wood rods had often been shaped on a diagonal so that two pieces could simply be laid against

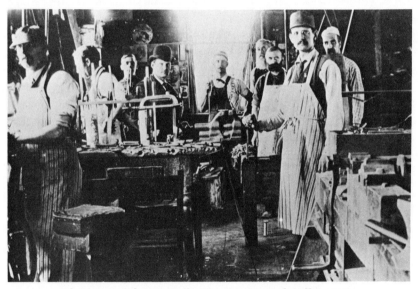

The Leonard-Hawes factory in Central Valley, NY,
pictured here during the 1890s, was not generally
open to photographers. Hiram Leonard's beveler,
once the most closely guarded secret of the rod-building
world, was hidden in a separate and locked double-doored room.
Entrance to that room meant immediate dismissal to
otherwise trusted employees.
(Photo donated by Mrs. Elsie Hawes to The Museum of
American Fly Fishing)

each other and spliced together with cord. You recall that back in Cotton's day, rods often were made in many pieces so that they could be left bound together during the entire season but completely dismantled for storage once it was over.

Ferrules are more than simple joints. They must be made to allow an even flexing of the rod, must be easily taken apart and, ideally, should be waterproof. The latter quality took considerable engineering and resulted in some rather unique schemes. Like the rest of the rod, the ferrule does a complex job in what appears to be a simple situation.

Guides found on today's fly rods are mainly simple wire "snakes" in combination with a hard tip guide of some sort and a first or stripping guide of agate, stainless steel, glass, carbide, or more recently, aluminum oxide or a similar material. At first there were some loosely-mounted rings that would simply "lie down" if the rod stood vertical. Then there were more ornate guides of a bridge type that stayed with bait rods but were too heavy for fly casting.

Varnish helped make a finished rod attractive, and durability during weathering and flexing was the product of endless research. At first, split-bamboo rods were rounded so that the flat faces didn't show, but this obviously reduced strength through loss of some important exterior fibers, so the flat surfaces were left on later models.

Fine split-bamboo rods were not turned out like hoe handles. Only a few top lines were ever made. Thus most of the early rod builders were rather retiring types who were not interested in public relations. This carried on into the late 20th century, the great craftsmen avoiding publicity and sometimes keeping construction methods secret from each other.

In reading *Classic Rods and Rodmakers* by Martin J. Keane, I was delighted at his tales of difficulty in interviewing the great rod builders, even those of the present day. Keane, recognized as one of the top bamboo rod authorities, invested a small fortune in travel in order to gather material for his text. Apparently the great rod builder, like any other artist, is likely to be more interested in the product than in its advertising or promotion.

You may find that glass or graphite better fills your need but you can see that a host of variables are involved in a top-grade Leonard or Winston rod. The final function may appear relatively simple, but

the fine bamboo fly rod involves advanced engineering, persnick-
ety workmanship and a knowledge of what the rod is supposed to do.
If he himself can't cast, the prospective rod designer doesn't have
much chance.

Many a "dream rod" has been broken over the builder's knee when
his theories didn't work out or materials failed him. Like other great
workmen, he is likely to "wear a hole in the floor" at his bench.

In the early days, rod-making machinery was improvised from
dreams and much of it was kept secret. Perhaps most of it could be
bought today, but rod-making gadgets are not turned out like lawn-
mowers. Keane tells us that most of the employees in the old Leonard
factory weren't even allowed in the beveling room.

Charles F. Murphy of Newark, New Jersey, evidently made the first
split-bamboo rods "for the trade." He's credited with a split-bamboo
salmon rod in 1865 and made what's believed to be the first split-
bamboo bass rod in 1866. When we say "bass rod" we mean one
intended for throwing bait with a turning reel. Bear with me on
these terms because they're all we have. When the man first named it
a baitcasting rod he didn't know it would also be used for plugs
and spinnerbaits.

There are a number of really famous bamboo fly rods that came
and went with the economy and the desires of anglers. The names, of
course, are those of original builders of long ago. In some cases later
bearers of the great names have reached for the fast buck and
cheapened their rods, but that's not the picture in general. The reason is that those who want "good lumber," as slangy casters have put
it, are willing to pay for it and are likely to be good judges.

In early 1980 a rod with one of the old names might have cost
around $750. Dollars don't mean much in light of inflation and defla-
tion, but in 1980 a medium-priced automobile cost about $9000.
Taking that as a measuring stick, I have done a layman's "guessti-
mation" of what actual rod costs would have been 100 years ago.

A rod offered by John Krider of Philadelphia in 1878, estimating
labor hours and materials *at 1980 levels,* would have cost $1800 the
way I figure it. So the good old days weren't all bargains. Another cost
accounting can be done regarding the E.F. Payne rod that Theodore
Gordon reportedly traded 45 dozen flies for. If the flies cost $1.25 each
(not an unusual 1980 price), that would bring the rod to $675. So
top-notch split bamboos have always been luxuries.

Like many other specialized manufacturing businesses, the early rod building was centered in a small area, mostly near Maine. Hiram Leonard was best known of all the early makers. He was a highly erudite civil engineer, and because of health problems spent much of his early life in the Maine woods. He was born at Sebec.

Leonard made himself a fishing rod about 1870-71, when engaged as a gunsmith at Bangor. His first efforts were of ash and lancewood. A sporting goods house, Bradford and Anthony of Boston, liked his rods and engaged him to work in split bamboo. He started out making four-strip rods.

The plot of famous rod building thickens with the men who worked with Leonard. Some of the famous names associated with his at Bangor and at a plant in Central Valley, New York, were Hiram and Loman Hawes, E.W. Edwards, F.E. Thomas, George Varney and Ed Payne.

All of these were top rod men and collectors love to speculate upon the borrowing they did from each other's methods as they moved through rather involved combinations of rod companies. Just which

One of the Charles Murphy rods in the collection
of The Museum of American Fly Fishing.
There are less than ten of Murphy's rods known to exist.
(Photo courtesy of The Museum of American Fly Fishing, Inc.)

rod builder figured out what is a little vague, but they did set the trends in rod building. Their names lasted long after they were gone, often with family descendants in the same line of work. Reuben Leonard, Ed Mills and Hiram Hawes were successful tournament casters, and all were rod builders.

Some of the more delicate works of the 19th century builders actually competed in weight with the graphite rods that came later. For example, one of the Leonards made in 1894 was 8 feet, 2 inches long and weighed 2 ounces.

At one time or another, most of the large tackle companies produced split-bamboo rods, some of them employing famous rod builders as supervisors, designers or workmen. For example, the respected Kosmic rods were built by Thomas, Edwards and Payne for the United States Net and Twine Company, beginning about 1898.

Edwin C. Powell presented his first rod catalog in 1919 and located in Marysville, California, shortly afterward. He created a semi-hollow rod in 1931 and Powell rods became tournament winners.

The Winston rod got its name from Robert Winther and Lew Stoner, who built it in San Francisco beginning in 1927. About 1936, Stoner invented a fluted, hollow rod, giving tremendous casting power with light weight. Although the Winston people made equally fine rods for other purposes, they gained much of their reputation from tournament casters, several of whom held national records. The 1980 owner of the Winston concern was Tom Morgan of Montana, who continued building bamboo rods as well as glass and graphite. Doug Merrick, a master craftsman who had been with Winston since World War II, worked with Morgan as he got started.

Casting competition had been dominated by the East in its early years, but Western casters came on strongly at about the time of the Winston and Powell rods. Distance fly events were especially strong along the Pacific coast, partly because of the interest in steelheading, which placed a premium on long throws in the heavy mountain rivers.

The Charles F. Orvis Company requires special attention because of its leadership in impregnated bamboo and because of its long tenure as a sporting goods concern.

Charles Orvis founded his company in Manchester, Vermont, in 1856. In the late 1930s, D.C. Corkran bought the company from two sons of Charles Orvis. Wesley Jordan, rod designer and exhibition caster, became superintendent of the Orvis shop in 1940. By 1946 the Bakelite impregnated rods were in production.

The impregnation business was controversial at first. Some said it hindered the rod's action, and it did add a little weight, but it made the rods incredibly rugged. Also, the impregnated rod did not require varnish, having a weatherproof and satin-like finish.

When I was fooling with my first impregnated Orvis and examining a sample section of the material, fiberglass was just beginning to remake the rod industry. A salesman from another company commented succinctly:

"Hell, Corkran and Jordan have it made. The rod is expensive

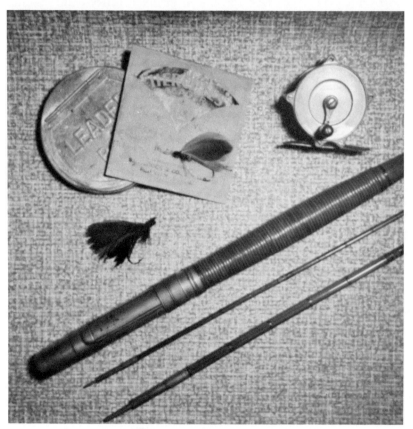

H.L. Leonard fly rod of about 1875 and a Leonard
raised-pillar fly reel (1877).
(Photo by Warren Shepard)

enough that fishermen will be careful with it anyway, and it's tougher than glass. It'll last forever."

The rod was a success all right, and still is. If there is any objection to the Orvis bamboo rods it's simply that there are too many of them to please collectors. Leigh Perkins, a direct-mail wizard, bought Orvis in 1965 and everything about it grew. It's still in Manchester.

Some of the very oldest of the fine split-bamboo rods are valued collector's items, but advanced technology, better tools, glue and finishing materials gave later makers an advantage.

Among connoisseurs of fine rods, some of the later models bring the highest prices of all (except in cases of extreme rarity). Two of the most valued rod types were produced in this century—the Gillums and the Garrisons.

H.C. "Pinky" Gillum, who built mostly custom rods, began learning

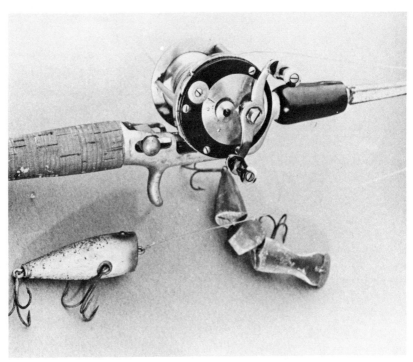

True Temper made this solid steel rod with an
excellent locking reel seat. The reel is a Shakespeare
Marhoff of the same era. Lures are Creek Club Plunker and
the jointed Heddon Game Fisher.

his skills in the 1920s, getting the elements of rod construction from E.W. Edwards, who was then supervising rod production at the Winchester rod shop in New Haven, Connecticut.

Edmund Everett Garrison's rods are the most valuable of all, according to most collectors. His production began early in the 1930s and he made about 700 rods, according to Martin Keane.

Many of the other older bamboo rods are excellent. In most cases the famous builders have merited their prominence, but there have undoubtedly been unsung geniuses who have built exceptionally fine rods, professionally or as a hobby.

While the fly rod developed and made reputations for those who built it, the other kinds of rods went in all directions. The most famous of bait rods was the Henshall bass rod, which was of modest length for its time. It was originated by James A. Henshall all right, but it appeared in so many variations that I'm inclined to consider Henshall more of an idea man than a rod builder.

The idea was to have a rod of around 8 feet long that would throw bait from a turning-spool reel and be balanced about like a somewhat longer trout rod.

Artists, even while illustrating sporting publications, have frequently been careless about the location of reels on rods. The confusion, of course, comes from the baitcasting reel being *on top* of the rod and the fly reel customarily being below. When I first saw illustrations of casting method of the Henshall days, I noted that the cast was made with the reel on top, but pictures of anglers playing fish showed it below the rod.

In a book written in 1918, Larry St. John explains that although the cast was made with the reel on top, it was then turned under for any further use. Sure enough, the casting illustrations show the reel handle on the left side so that a right-hander would have it properly suspended when he fished with it hanging down.

Here are some specifications of one Henshall model, highly approved by its namesake:

Made by Leonard of split bamboo, the rod was 8 feet, 1 inch long. The length of the grip was 6 inches and the diameter of the extreme tip was 3/32 of an inch. Weight was 6½ ounces. There were similar dimensions for other Henshall rods made from other materials, but these rods were somewhat heavier. The "standard" was of ash and lancewood.

With his rod, Henshall said he could "easily cast a minnow from 40 to 50 yards, and with great accuracy."

Henshall had a great knowledge of fish and fishing and I tend to dig out one of his books when seeking fishing information of his time. So when I snipe a little at his opinions, I do so in humility. After all, I've had 100 years of second-guessing to chortle over.

Anyway, the man who shortened and lightened the "baitcasting" rod got a fixation at about 8 feet. He didn't go for artificial lures and maintained that casting should be done in a soft sweep from the side, a good drill for delicate baits. When there was a move toward the graceful and accurate 6-footer of a later day, Henshall resisted bitterly. Said he:

". . . There has arisen a new departure in black bass rods that out-Herods Herod. Rods—we must call them so by courtesy—are now made from 4 to 6 feet long for casting the live frog or pork rind in boat fishing. The casting is done overhead and forward, as in fly fishing, and the frog, being reeled up to the tip, is projected in the manner of throwing a small apple from the end of a slender stick."

Henshall admitted the method made for accuracy but complained that the rod was very short and very stiff (the "Chicago" rod was this type) and didn't give the fish a chance. He goes on:

"This mode of angling, however, does not appeal to one who has a just appreciation of the amenities of the gentle art and a love for suitable tackle. . . ."

But the shorter rod was on its way. It is said that it was introduced on the casting platform by Lloyd Tooley and Tilden Robb.

Steel rods for both bait and fly casting were around in the 1890s. The leading supplier was Horton Manufacturing Company. Those steel rods were hollow tubes with a "crack" lengthwise. The seam wasn't welded and aided the rod's flexing. Even in an 1894 Montgomery Ward catalog there was a Bristol that telescoped. They were heavy but worked better than you'd guess.

Steel held on until after World War II (when fiberglass arrived), the various alloys giving different actions. Best known of the high-grade metal rods was the True Temper, built by the American Fork and Hoe people. It was hollow, lightweight and tapered in smooth stepdowns, and actually pretty attractive. But there was trouble with all very light metal rods. Corrosion or rust was insidious and the walls had to be very thin to keep the weight down. The True Temper rod was used by some accuracy casting champions and was lovingly repaired when broken—a pretty complicated business, but indicative of the fact that steel certainly wasn't all bad.

The real brutes were the solid steel models made by a number of companies. They were heavy but capable of good plug casting. All were too heavy for fly fishing.

The real plugging rods started about 1900 as artificial lures for bass and pike began to appear everywhere. Americans who toast Jim Heddon's invention tend to ignore the British artificial minnows which had been around since Walton's friendly seamstress produced them from a living model. But most of those weren't intended for true casting. They were trolled, or "spinned."

The principle of casting a lure with the line running through guides

In an age of mass-produced tackle there is still
a place for careful hand work.
Tom Morgan of the Winston Rod Company here does
finishing work on fine split-bamboo fly rods.

has been around for a long time. Clear back in 1682 Thomas Nobbes of Britain said he could cast 20 yards by running line through a ring at the tip of his rod, not using a reel at all. Very light lures were "strip casted" with fly rods for many years before modern spinning (stationary spool) virtually wiped out the practice.

Many materials and tricky names were tried to get the rod market of 1900 and thereabouts. In advertising, as later, there was emphasis upon extreme strength. The "steel-ribbed" rods were tastefully wrapped with wire and the "steel-centered" rods had a steel core. Some steel rods were flexible enough that the rod tip could be tied in a knot. Though this had little to do with the rods' fishing qualities, it was a potent sales gimmick. Early bamboo was called "steel vine."

Even in the 1970s, extreme strength of glass and graphite was touted in demonstrations in which a rod was used to tow a cabin cruiser. Never mind that cabin cruisers are unusual catches. It sold rods.

While the masters of rod building stayed in the background, hundreds of trick materials and methods competed for public acceptance around the 20th century's beginning. Strangely, split bamboo would not go away.

CHAPTER FIVE

THE REELS

No matter how carefully histo-
rians try to avoid the subject, there is a great void in American sport
fishing history, some 200 years during which little was reported
about it.

That period was roughly from the time the colonists first gained a
solid foothold in their New World until some time in the 19th century.
Let's try to explain it away.

The French and Spanish settlers apparently took no interest in
sport fishing. I say "apparently" because if they wrote much about it
we never found their records. Remember that only the more important things got into translations, so it's not likely their notations about
bluefish or trout would have appeared in English.

Until the Revolutionary War, Mother England stifled American fishing developments, not deliberately, but as effectively as if there had
been laws. You see, all sports were in the traditions of the mother
countries. The British aristocracy fished for trout and salmon, partly
with flies and otherwise with tackle similar to fly equipment of the
time. It is doubtful if anyone thought of making a gamefish of a

striped bass or a muskellunge, and if he did he probably kept pretty quiet about it. Since those were "new" fish, they didn't really count.

America's own development of fishing equipment was to be keyed to the black bass, a fish that was misnamed. It was completely misunderstood and located mostly on the edges of early settlement, not being present along the most rapidly developing coastal areas. But until Americans started bass fishing they didn't seem to have many new ideas of their own. The English ways were good enough—and often unattainable for pioneers in a new land.

I think Washington Irving, evidently no fisherman at all, made an interesting contribution to this historical vacuum. Irving assimilated a great deal of Izaak Walton's works and, like many other literary people, was completely captivated by it. So intriguing were the visions of rural England that Irving and a party of friends decided to transplant the contemplative joys of angling to America.

The B.C. Milam reels were among the finest of
the "Kentuckies." This one, made about 1870, did not employ
a counterbalance on the handle.

This was one of the first of thousands of humorous, semi-humorous and completely non-humorous accounts of greenhorns venturing into fishing. Of course everything went wrong and Irving concluded that fishing should be done in England where there was "rule and system" and where "every roughness has been softened away from the landscape."

I think that tells most of the story. Here we have residents of a frontier country deploring the virgin wilds and pining for the "softened" landscape of England, where Walton and Cotton could rest in their fishing hut on the Dove, and where the scenery was shaped by centuries of agriculture.

Most of the American fishing was to be in less "softened" surroundings, the part now desired most by most Americans. Desire for wild country is not confined to any nationality, although it is true that American fishermen often present a cruder facade than English ones. Let's face the fact, a little class distinction still sneaks into the European fishing bit.

Just a few years ago, a British landowner, when approached about a leasing arrangement that would give Americans a chance at his fishing water, said he'd "just as soon have a herd of warthogs as a bunch of Yanks on my stream." He said it in good nature and for all I know the lease was consummated, but the democratic Americans sometimes behave in a way that would discourage Walton. All of this, we are told, comes from fishing on unlimited waters. Of course, they are no longer unlimited.

At any rate, it was the beginning of the 19th century before Americans began to make a mark in fishing tackle. The important part started with the Kentucky reel, a precision mechanism that began in the bluegrass country in the general area of Lexington. It's strange that the Kentucky rifle and the Kentucky reel would influence sport at about the same time. But the Kentucky rifle was generally made in Pennsylvania, acquiring its name because the "hunters of Kentucky" used it in its various forms and "Kentucky" embodied all that was felt about the frontier, bringing out visions of eagle-eyed outdoorsmen.

Although the first maker of a Kentucky reel had come from Pennsylvania, the reel was invented in Kentucky and made there for almost half a century before it received much recognition elsewhere. We can generalize and say that the Germans who settled in Pennsylvania were very skilled craftsmen.

Daniel Boone had first settled in frontier Kentucky in 1775, only 25 years or so before the first precision reels were designed. It may seem an unusual site for such work, but we had a special situation: well-heeled sportsmen without salmon or trout to fish for. They had shed Europe's traditions to some extent. They had their own culture and some new gamefish, especially the black bass.

The first rods purely for black bass fishing were used differently from those that went with the Kentucky reels. In 1764 Bartram wrote of use of a "bob" for bass in Florida. There is no indication of how long it had been used, or if Indians might have used a similar rig for centuries.

It was not considered a sporting method and was scorned by the first writers on recreational fishing. It is still used in the South, still catches some big bass, is perfectly legal in most areas, and whether it is sporting or not is up to the individual fisherman. It has gone by several names. "Jiggerbobbing" is a popular one as is simply "bobbing." I've also heard it called "doodlesocking," "jigger fishing" and several other things. In recent years a detailed course in it together with somewhat refined equipment has sold at high prices as a sort of miracle method.

The original bobs, as described by Bartram, were made of three large hooks lashed together (making a "treble") and carried a big wad of white hair from a deer's tail, along with assorted feathers. This was fastened with some 20 inches of heavy line to the tip of a 10- or 12-foot pole. One angler paddled a canoe and the other waved the lure about near the water, touching it down occasionally, according to the early account.

There are, of course, different versions. I suspect the most refined and most commonly practiced by present day experts involves keeping the lure and tip of the pole in the water almost constantly rather than waving them about. The idea is that the turbulence of the water caused by the pole's tip and the lure will keep the fish from noticing the boat.

The "bob" has often been replaced by fish strips, large pieces of pork rind, spoons and plugs. One prized lure was made of leather in the silhouette of a small alligator. Once hooked, the fish is generally brought in by hand-over-handing the rod, since the short line doesn't work well with landing nets. The method is similar to "figure-eight-ing," which usually involves wire lines and has been done from sundry saltwater piers and bridges with a variety of lures, including glass insulators from telephone poles.

"Bobbing," or whatever you want to call it, is frequently confused with "skittering," which is a similarly ancient craft. In skittering, the fisherman uses a lighter pole and a considerably longer line to "skitter" a spoon, spinner or other lure or bait along the surface.

Both of these early methods are important because they are the beginning of moving artificial lures for bass not involving trolling. Either could be used with a reel but rarely were and rarely are, even today. Both are at their best in weedy waters where normal "playing" of fish is impractical.

The Kentucky live-bait system with precision reels was something entirely different.

Even the first of the Kentucky reels was a long step from the great wooden Nottingham reels favored in England, and similar reels in other countries, used mainly for line storage and fish playing.

A watchmaker named George Snyder of Paris, Kentucky (near Lexington), made one of the first and probably the first of the Kentucky reels between 1800 and 1810. The reel was a quadruple mul-

Wooden Nottingham reel was a durable forerunner of modern "winches." There were many inexpensive wooden reels of less quality.

tiplying model that Snyder made for himself and for friends, members of his angling club. Then Jonathan Meek, also a watchmaker, produced reels commercially, beginning around 1833. Meek reels remained famous for more than 100 years, becoming collector's prizes. About 1840 Jonathan Meek formed a partnership with his brother Benjamin F. Meek.

Other names in the development were B.G. Milam, a Meek apprentice who brought improvements, and J.W. Hardman of Louisville, who introduced screws to take the place of rivets. Meek reels were assembled with numbered screws prior to 1845. Later, there was a move to takedowns without tools. Most of the first reels were made of brass with square steel gears; Meek began to bevel them around 1860. Nickel, or German silver, appeared after the Civil War.

The purpose of the quadruple multiplier was ease in casting—the spool had "leverage" against the handle and thus turned easier. A hundred years later, the multiplying feature was considered essential for lure manipulation, but there is surprisingly little mention of it concerning the retrieve in early accounts. Dr. James A. Henshall, the

Fine casting reels from another age.
L. to R.: V.L. & A. reel with oversized jewelled bearings,
Meek No. 33 Blue Grass and Julius vom Hofe (pat., 1885).

most highly recognized bass authority of that century, felt a fast retrieve was of little importance, and even hinted it was unsportsmanlike to crank in a fish too swiftly.

Jewelled bearings helped make the reels run smoothly, and although they may not have become common until much later, Henshall states that the "personal and favorite" reel of George Snyder, made in 1810, had garnet jewel bearings. Adjustable clicks appeared early. Handles were counterbalanced and the spool length or "reel width" varied considerably, even as it did in much later models.

The early reels had heavy spools. The theory of light spools for reduction of overrun (causing backlash) evidently was not considered for a long time, though by 1905 aluminum spools were available in Meek reels. Some Kentucky reels were showpieces. B.F. Meek built one of solid silver with a tuned "bell click" for a New Orleans artist about 1846.

How were the first Kentuckies used? They were used for casting minnows, and so the term "baitcasting" has plagued and confused artificial lure throwers to this day. The casting method is well documented, a rather light native cane rod was used, lighter than a heavy-duty salmon fly rod. The reels were lashed on or attached with screws.

The caster threw the bait in a sweeping, sidearm motion using one hand, a good way to deliver a minnow. Any snap casting would destroy the bait, which was probably alive and hooked through the mouth or back. If there was any "spinning" (moving the natural bait through the water at considerable speed, as done by the British) it certainly was not common. By mid-century spoons and spinners were available, but the cast-and-retrieve process hadn't caught on. Artificials were generally used for trolling.

The natural cane rods of the Kentucky innovators were about 10 feet long. These rods were later replaced by other materials, but for bait fishing the combination was highly satisfactory; very similar tackle was used through much of the next century. Here was soft delivery of a delicate bait for considerable distance.

For about 70 years, the new reels were used mostly near their place of creation. Modifications of the Kentucky design did work into other kinds of angling, but bass fishing didn't change much. That was a long time coming.

The Kentucky country had exceptional fishing, not only for bass but also for walleye and muskellunge. Early changes in the waters occurred as dams began to appear and the population grew, but fishing methods there went on rather isolated from other parts of the country. No outdoor magazines or television programs existed to show fishermen the fine points of any area.

The precision reel had no tradition behind it, of course, and was completely new in concept. And it's strange that this reel came into being as a live bait thrower because precision was less needed for the long, soft casting rods than for the quicker snap casting of a later day.

Farther north a somewhat different approach to the bass business was taken, and the somewhat shorter and very stiff "Chicago rod" came along. Casting in that locale seems to have centered around the natural frog chunked into weedy waters. Fishermen were still groping for rod and reel combinations.

Brass multiplying reels had been common by 1770. Apparently the double-multiplier satisfied most fishermen. The quad was not recog-

The Orvis 1874 fly reel was the first
commercial reel to combine the elements of the modern fly reel:
a narrow, ventilated spool mounted upright on the seat.
The reel sold for $3.00 in its walnut box.

nized as a breakthrough and worked right along with slower mechanisms. At various times experiments were conducted with much faster retrieves, but anything more than a quad gave the fish considerable leverage, and playing fish seemed to take precedence over any kind of casting.

Some makers pointed out that a narrow but deep spool could give a much faster takeup than a long, shallow one. Fly fishermen tended to use the same reels that went for bait fishing, generally with a fairly wide spool and of a multiplying design. Multiplying fly reels of more advanced design had some popularity again by the 1970s, but the traditional fly reel was single-actioned.

A hundred years ago, James A. Henshall neatly classified fishing reels as multipliers, click reels and automatics. The click reels, sometimes beautifully made, were used for all kinds of fishing—in single action. It's a little confusing that the multipliers might also have clicks. Before anti-backlash devices, some casters threw with the click on.

When Charles Orvis produced his fly reel it was a rather obvious advancement, having a deep, narrow spool that carried considerable line, took up rapidly, and spooled fly line in such large loops that kinking was avoided. It was also ventilated, a great help to silk line. Such line still needed to be taken off and dried after each trip, but it was much better off stored on the Orvis ventilated spool than on one with no ventilation at all.

Although Orvis put his ventilated reel on the market in 1874 and the trend in fly reels was definitely toward the silhouette, baitcasting type reels were still being used by some fly casters in the 1920s. Orvis also perfected a minnow trap (for shame!) that saw use almost unchanged for generations.

Automatic reels for fly fishing have been around for a century. Some of the first were scary mechanisms that fascinated lovers of things mechanical. Then, in later years, more compact, lighter models appeared that served beautifully for many kinds of fly fishing, though somewhat scorned by traditionalists. Of course the automatic doesn't work for long-running fish, but it is invaluable for keeping coils of fly line from underfoot when the fish are smaller. Still, traditionalists would rather strangle in excess line than use one.

Reel developments, like those of firearms, never followed a logical sequence. Just as muzzleloading firearms were preferred by many long after cartridges became practical, so certain kinds of primitive reels remained on the market long after there were precision casting tools. For example, wooden reels held on into the 20th century. A frequently mentioned English reel, the Nottingham, was popular in both England and America and an example of it, made of walnut and mounted in brass, appears in an 1890s Foster's catalog from England. Innumerable less expensive wooden reels from all over the world are scorned by some of the more selective of today's tackle collectors.

"Raised-pillar" reels, single-actioned or multiplying, have been used off and on by fly fishermen for a long while. Although not as trim in appearance as round models, they have obvious advantages. The raised pillars simply hold together a frame somewhat larger than the spool, adding slightly to line capacity. If the spool is filled the added space around it allows somewhat sloppy spooling. I suspect its sale was somewhat hampered by presence of some very cheap models.

In a piece about rodmaker Hiram Lewis Leonard in *The American Fly Fisher,* Mary Kefover Kelly tells of a raised-pillar fly reel patented by Leonard's business associate, Frances J. Philbrook. It has since been called the Leonard reel and the patent, issued in 1877, was assigned to Leonard.

Nickel-plated and German-silver casting reels largely replaced plain brass. Hard-rubber endplates were admittedly more fragile than those of metal, but persisted in some very expensive fly and saltwater trolling models. Hard rubber (or a plastic much like it) was found in some of the finest salmon fly reels up to the 1980s.

Although historians of fly fishing make much of earlier fly reels, they weren't especially important in laying out line or playing small- to medium-size fish of the 19th century. The largest fish consistently sought by fly fishermen were Atlantic salmon, and although they make long runs the reels used for them were not required to withstand the strains of saltwater fish weighing more than 100 pounds. Precise as they were, those fine salmon reels were replaced by simpler and heavier bar-stock aluminum single actions when big tarpon and billfish were sought by later generations.

At first, baitcasters relied completely on their "educated" thumbs to prevent backlash. Little or no effort was made to mechanically control the spool. Most fishermen seemed to ignore the "flywheel" tendencies of a heavy spool, and were instead impressed by one that would spin for a long time after a flick of the handle. Then there came jewelled bearings that could be adjusted to slow things down.

"Anti-backlash" devices soon appeared in abundance. One of the earlier ones was a sort of wire bail that dropped down on the spinning spool and slowed the cast. Probably the best known of those was the South Bend, which appeared long after other methods had been used. By 1923 the South Bend anti-backlash device was being combined with a level-wind. On today's light reels, centrifugal force pushes tiny braking devices against a smooth surface. The Penn Squidder, a long-term favorite of surf casters, has internal "fan blades" that slow the spool as the speed becomes too great.

Level-wind was a feature which began early and took a long time to become popular. Henshall says the first level-wind was made by Wheeler & McGregor of Milwaukee. Anyway, level-winds were in use around the turn of the century on baitcasting reels. This gadget was

Early Yawman & Erbe automatic fly reel (left) and
a skeleton-type fly reel of the 1880s.

handicapped somewhat by the deprecation of veteran fishermen who felt anyone who couldn't spool his own line evenly was something of a greenhorn.

Two general types of level-winding mechanism were used. One was a rather long "finger" with a line aperture that swung back and forth in front of the spool. The other was an "eye" that traveled left and right on a worm gear, much as with the modern designs. There were even some inexpensive level-wind attachments that could be used with reels originally built without them. But even after World War II, light baitcasting reels with no level-wind were still in use, especially by tournament casters.

With the early rods there was less need for level-wind because the sticks were so heavy it was necessary to place one hand ahead of the reel during a retrieve. When lighter rod materials came along, together with shorter baitcasting tips, it was more efficient to cup the reel in the hand. Because saltwater rods for heavier fishing require two hands, the pawl-and-worm level-wind never really did become

Australia's Alvey reel works much as the old Malloch did, although considerably refined. White reel is set for casting, black one for retrieve.

popular there. Today, some surf reels have a curved pillar to guide the line on properly.

I'm afraid modern manufacturers have retrogressed in one field, that of the "Take-A-Part" reels. I once thought it was a term applied exclusively to a Meisselbach model I coveted as a youth, but I find the phrase was used for a number of high-grade casting reels around 1900 and somewhat later. Some of those advertised then were the "President," produced by Julius vom Hofe (a forerunner of the Meisselbach I never was able to afford), a Manhattan, a Blue Grass and an American model.

Those reels were rather simply made and when later builders applied more gadgetry including level-winds, complex gearing, drags and centrifugal speed control, the quick takedown without tools just wasn't practical.

I believe one of the strongest movements in development of the heavy-duty reel as well as the first thrust into true saltwater sport fishing came during a 40-year period, roughly from the end of the Civil War to the beginning of the new century. New England striped bass clubs, not too well known by modern fishermen, were responsible for this development. The Kentucky black bass reels were too small for salt water, but their construction undoubtedly had an influence.

The club casters, operating from elevated stands, could afford the best. Their reels were precise, although freespooling and the star drag were yet to be perfected, at least for most of the striper club era. It was almost time for sportsmen to invade the open sea and they would need better winches. "Winch" was a common early name for the reel, not intended as slang.

Without practical drags, the thumbstall or "cot" was a necessity, sometimes worn on both thumbs, for the best of the stand casters were capable of lobbing their baits to either right or left at the instant feeding fish were sighted. The striper clubmen demonstrated that the turning spool could cast large baits.

Necessity crowded invention strongly after Dr. C.F. Holder caught his tuna of 183 pounds in 1898. Holder and others of his time really breached the invisible barrier between shore-bound rod and reel fishermen and true deep-water angling. I like the comment made by Harlan Major in his book on saltwater angling. He says, "—the most important part of his equipment consisted of unlimited courage

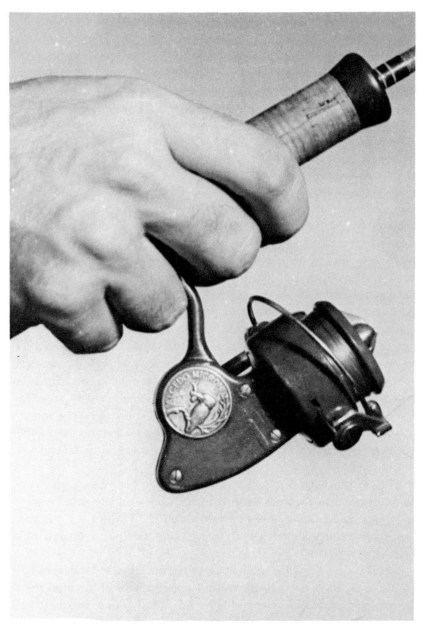

*Ultra-light spinning became an obsession when fine lines
and reels became available.
This tiny model is the famed Alcedo Micron.*

backed up by a powerful fireproof thumb. Outgoing line spun the reel handle backwards with the viciousness of a buzzsaw."

William Boschen took some ideas to Julius vom Hofe, a Brooklyn reel maker who did some machining. Boschen worked also with Joe Coxe, then in 1913 caught a broadbill swordfish with a reel using an internal drag having a 3-plate multiple-disk clutch and a handle that turned only forward. These devices had been around for some time, but the swordfish evidently prompted their popularity.

Incidentally, a leather thumb tab attached to a reel pillar came into use without fanfare. It was probably too simple for attention. It took the place of a thumbstall to some extent but either or both could become warm in a hurry. What we call the "star drag" has been credited to Edward vom Hofe, who caught a record tarpon weighing 210 pounds and had found it hard on his thumb brake.

Chronology is difficult in following reel development. The star drag got its name simply from the star-shaped adjustment "knob" under the reel handle. Most drags used in playing fish are metal discs with washers made of leather, plastic or fiber. They were greatly improved almost immediately after they went to sea. The simple drag handles for baitcasting reels used in heavy fishing (the "cub" handle was well known as an accessory) have been around in some form since the century began. The refinements of drags on both light and heavy tackle continued into the 1980s, although the basics remained much the same. Improvements were in materials and lubrication.

Really large offshore reels led the way in drag development and some of the first truly big ones were built by Joe Coxe for Zane Grey. He and the vom Hofe brothers were best known in the field.

Henshall, in his 1904 edition of the *Book of the Black Bass,* lists the following as the "principal manufacturers for the trade": Julius vom Hofe, Brooklyn; A.F. Meisselbach & Bro., Newark, New Jersey; The American Company, Rockford, Illinois; and the Andrew B. Hendrix Co., New Haven, Connecticut. He lists B.C. Milam and Son, Frankfort, Kentucky, and A.B. Meek & Sons of Louisville as prominent *custom* reel builders.

"Best known" and most successful builders do not necessarily make all of the best equipment. By its very nature, the custom, handmade reel must be made in small quantities and is likely to get little publicity. A collector may clutch to his bosom a reel the average sportsman has never heard of.

CHAPTER SIX

THE LURES

In the beginnings of sport fishing artificial lures weren't considered particularly important. They came along gradually, probably starting with the decoys used for spearing, then developing into jigs with hooks to be worked up and down through holes in the ice. Professional saltwater fishermen have used them for a long while and I find no record of their origin there. It probably was long before anybody made any written record of anything. The jig was to be used much differently later on.

Of course there were unweighted feature lures; we call them *flies.* The artificial minnow of Walton's day wasn't called a "plug." The term evidently didn't come into use until Jim Heddon whittled his cigar-shaped gadget about 1896.

At first all *plugs* were made of wood. The term "plugcasting" eventually included metal and plastic plugs once they became common. It is strange that the method of casting and retrieving a lure with built-in action developed so gradually as to be hardly mentioned. "Spinning," the business of moving a minnow through the water so that it revolved, was a prelude to the lure with integral action. And we got into terms such as *wobbler* and *wiggler.*

Wood was mentioned as lure material before the Civil War. R. Haskell's patent of 1859 was for a wood-bodied "Fish Hook" in the shape of a minnow. Pflueger patented "artificial fish baits" with luminous paint in 1883, some of which would have been called plugs had they appeared later.

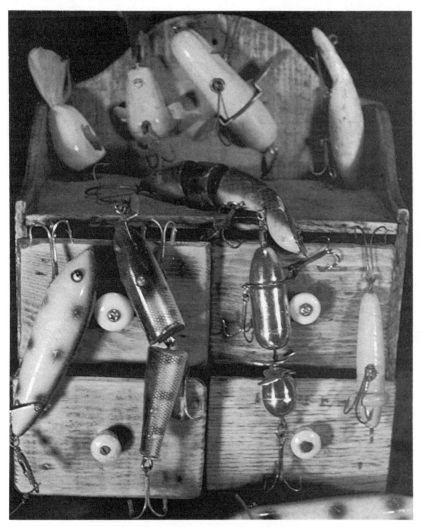

Antique Plugs of 1898 to 1925.
(Photo by Warren Shepard from the Heddon Collection)

British lures, the Phantom Minnow, the Devon Minnow and the "Devils" (strongly resembling Walton's imitation produced by the seamstress), began to appear in America quite early, but there isn't much information as to exactly how they were used. Some, of course, were trolled, and others manipulated with long rods. The Phantom was in use shortly after 1800, appearing at almost exactly the same time as the Kentucky reel—but I can't find the two used together. The Phantom stayed around and appeared in catalogs until the 1940s. A William Mills and Sons catalog shows it as made of rubber-coated silk, evidently too light for any kind of casting from a reel. A variety of sizes was available. Most Phantoms had metal heads and fins.

A surface "spinner" with an attached wooden float was patented by H.C. Brush in 1876, and may have been the first wooden lure actually to be manufactured.

Novelty baits have clung to the edges of the market almost from the beginnings of artificials. Abercrombie and Fitch marketed a soft-rubber mouse covered with "real skin" in 1907. The use of mice as lures for black bass and large trout is recounted in endless stories through the years. An ancient system of "mousing" for trout in moving water involved lashing a mouse to a hook and setting it adrift on a chip. When the miniature raft had reached the area thought to hold the trophy trout, the unfortunate mouse would be pulled overboard and its swimming efforts were likely to attract attention. Granted, a swimming mouse is not a routine resident of trout or bass water, but a great many mouse imitations have been marketed. Nestlings have been used frequently by angling ogres, but I find no imitation song-birds produced in early lures. There were some by 1980.

Some novelty baits of a later day were produced in the image of well-formed, back-stroking mermaids and beer bottles or cans. Less exotic numbers were adapted from tie clasps (the South Bend Super Duper) and the wooden clothespin (Porter Seahawk).

The "clothespin bait" rates attention for its special application. With the line attached somewhat back of the weighted "head," the clothespin was remarkably effective when worked from a bridge or fishing pier in salt water. The best known, the Seahawk, balanced and retrieved much like a jig, became very popular by the 1950s. A similar lure, the "Pinhead," appeared in catalogs in the 1930s.

From time to time there have been self-propelled lures and others with mechanical fin and tail wiggles. Electrically lighted baits have been designed repeatedly. One designer worked hard on an explosive lure that would blow the fish's brains out, but told me in 1956 he had worked out no method of landing the dead catch.

Weird novelty baits have had brief spasms of popularity. One set of lures sold at county fairs during the 1950s involved rubber frog, worm or minnow imitations with long, slender hoses that ran up to the rod handle and were equipped with squeeze bulbs. Squeeze the bulb and your frog or minnow would swim. Your rubber worm would writhe.

Some of the more practical "advanced" systems of the 1980s had ancestors long ago. In 1914 there was at least one application which involved "variable" line connections on plugs. The line could be attached at different points for different depths or actions, same as a popular "innovation" of much later.

Spoons may have been used almost as long as jigs. The dates of their discovery among South Sea islanders by various Europeans

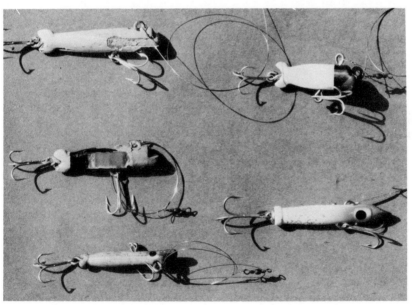

Stages in development of a popular lure, the Porter Seahawk,
known as a "clothespin" lure.

really give no idea how long primitive people may have used them. The spoon-shaped object is a natural wobbler in the water and some of the aboriginal fishermen simply altered a seashell so that it had a built-in hook. They could troll it behind their canoes, cast it with handlines or use it as a jig.

Seashells have such a variety of colors and so much iridescence that they certainly didn't need paint. Today we have metal spoons in mother-of-pearl and abalone finishes. Just for fun I have used ordinary seashell spoons with hooks attached. They're easy to make although the exact action is hard to predict.

Trade names are essential in defining the beginning of some *types* of lures. A first maker has a head start and deserves special credit, even though some later design might prove superior.

There's nothing vague about the beginning of fishing spoon manufacture in America. It's agreed that it started with Julio Buel, a young furrier, who was trolling worms or minnows over dropoffs in a Vermont lake. In eating his lunch he dropped a silver spoon overboard and saw a big trout grab it as it flickered and wobbled toward the bottom. He told the story himself, although there have been disbelievers. Buel made a lure by soldering a hook to the concave part of another spoon, and experimented with various paints and the addition of feathers.

He sent some samples of his spoons to Frank Forester, an outdoor writer (his real name was Henry William Herbert), and got some good publicity. He started the J.T. Buel Company of Whitehall, New York, in 1848. From then on his firm never was able to fill its orders, even though he soon had some competitors. I guess it wouldn't be very easy to patent a derivation of a tablespoon.

There were other spoons made in nearly the same image as the Buel. A Pflueger luminous spoon was patented in 1880, and confusing terminology arose regarding spoons and spinners. Some of the "spoons" such as the popular feathered models were built to revolve around a shaft. The fluted turning spoons of Skinner, Pflueger and Buel were look-alikes, and that type may have caught more muskellunge and pike than any other.

The Skinner spoon became famous about 1870, a time when muskellunge fishing came into its own in the St. Lawrence River area. A feathered treble hook of appropriate size was attached to most of these lures.

Since it turned around a shaft, it's hard to see why some descriptive distinction wasn't made between the wobbling and turning spoons. Spoon-shaped attractors remain popular. When they get small and turn they are generally called "spinners." Big ones are still "spoons." Other spinners were shaped like airplane propellers, often in tandem, and the spinners mounted on plugs have been mostly of that kind.

Revolving and wobbling spoons, although completely different in action, both relied upon flash or glitter for their basic attraction. The wobbling spoon best known of all was (and is) the Dardevle, a creation of 1916-17. Lou Eppinger, who put it into production, said he was primarily interested in an effective casting lure that could be thrown by the tackle of that time without excessive backlashing.

Eppinger said most plugs available then were too light and bulky for casting with ordinary reels and that the Meek and Talbot reels were too fast for anyone except an expert. At the time, a light-action bait-

With the use of small lures, spinning came into its own.
These are tiny experimental lures and some bigger ones as
used with a small closed-face reel.

casting rod wasn't around yet. The live-bait throwers of Henshall's time were too long for real lure casting and there had been a radical departure to stiff rods of 3 to 4 feet. Even some of the split-bamboo rods of that time were poker-stiff. Short metal rods held on persistently in some parts of the country until late in the 1920s, and were a favorite of the Ozark Mountain fishermen until about 1930.

Eppinger was a Detroit taxidermist and sporting goods dealer. He tested his spoons as early as 1906 in Ontario, where the northern pike were thick. He first named his lure the Osprey, but after the First World War called it the Dare Devil, a name applied to the U.S. Marines. Church folks didn't like that bad word spelled out, so the name was changed to Dardevle, even though it was pronounced the same.

The Dardevle was easy to cast and it adapted to a wide variety of fishing methods. Given a little time to sink, it would go to considerable depth before the retrieve, and it had a peculiar attraction as it sank, swinging erratically from side to side and giving off a series of flashes. It was a good depth prospector. If fish struck it on the way down their depth was easily determined. As with many later designs, Dardevle casters often count as their bait sinks in order to establish the most profitable depth.

There is no record of how many spoons (usually less expensive) have been made in frank imitation of the Dardevle. Although the Eppinger firm has designed numerous other baits, the simple original is best known and for many years that type of spoon was simply called a "Daredevil," no matter who made it.

Controversy reigned. The originals were shaped for action and weight, the thickness varying over different parts of the lure. But it was possible for imitators to simply stamp them out at low cost, keeping the original outline with no regard to the thickness variations. The original Dardevles generally were durably finished with costly enamels. Some of the cheaper imitations got a lick and a promise.

Fishermen were admonished to beware of counterfeits and told that the original would catch many more fish. This wasn't all Dardevle advertising but became a preachment of numerous outdoor writers. Such a message still appears from time to time. Apparently, subtle differences exist in the actions which are important in some situations. In other kinds of fishing there might not be much difference. There is no doubt concerning the quality of finishes.

The Dardevle type of wobbling spoon is particularly well adapted to bank fishing of steep shorelines. It can be cast well out, allowed to sink almost to the shelving bottom and then retrieved at just the right speed to maintain its distance from that bottom. Spoon lovers also cast them into swift rivers and allow them to actually scrape, tinkle and grate along the rocky bottoms as they swing downstream during retrieve.

Lou Eppinger was succeeded by his nephew, Edward A. Eppinger, and the Dardevle continued to be used a great deal, especially by trout fishermen, Pacific salmon fishermen and pike and muskie anglers. By the 1950s there were so many spoons made in the general Dardevle outline that the market was greatly divided. Some other spoons of the same type might be superior in a specific situation, such as extremely thick metal for very fast sinking or paper-thin metal for extra "flutter." No one has ever doubted Dardevle quality.

The Johnson Silver Minnow, the invention of Louis Johnson of Chicago, has been around since about 1920. As far as I can learn the first ones were all silver. Later came other finishes, especially gold and black. The Johnson spoon was something new in that it was one of the most weedless attractors ever made. Its slender shape does not produce wide-sweeping darts, but its peculiar wobbling action is hampered little by addition of pork rind, pork chunk or pork frog. There have been variations, but the simple Silver Minnow with its weedguard and hook "growing" out of the spoon is best known.

Weedy lakes and river backwaters see more Johnson spoons than any other fishing areas. Adept manipulators can change reeling speeds to cause the spoon to gurgle along the surface and then drop seductively into open spaces in the vegetation.

Where spoons leave off and metal "squids" begin is indistinct. A great many saltwater spoons are built with integral hooks in the same general design of the Johnson spoon. It would be hard to run down their origins, but they tend to be narrower than the Johnson, which has served primarily in fresh water. Most saltwater spoons are used for trolling, while most Johnson spoons are used for casting.

When Jim Heddon started his plug business he not only inaugurated an era of fishing, he headed a procession of eager inventors who contrived baits ranging from deadly to ridiculous. Heddon whittled the magic gadget in about 1896.

The plug, like the spoon, was convenient for casting. It's a wonder that "wooden minnows" had not appeared before since metal and cloth had been imitating baitfish for a long while.

Heddon, president of the American Bee Keepers Association, was already an inventor when he made his first plug, having patented some processes for the bee business. The story goes that he was sitting on a log beside Dowagiac Creek, whittling on a piece of wood. He tossed it into the creek and a bass struck.

The earliest lures were whittled and painted by hand and given to Heddon's fishing friends. James Heddon and his sons, Charles and William, formed a company about 1898. In 1902 they moved out of the family kitchen and into a building in downtown Dowagiac. It was common to call the early plugs Dowagiacs.

I believe most fishermen think of the torpedo-type plug with spinners fore and aft when they think of early Heddon plugs. However, the very first ones had no spinners. They were of a slightly plump cigar shape and had slanted collars for action. "Collared" plugs made by several manufacturers were popular in the 1920s.

Along with artificial minnows, various devices were made for

Well-known to fishermen 75 years later, the "torpedo" type
of lure was produced very early by Heddon.
Dated 1905, these are the No. 150 (above) and the No. 100
Dowagiac Minnows. (Photo from the Heddon Collection)

holding a dead bait so it would revolve or at least perform erratically when retrieved or trolled. An extension of this came a little later in the form of an enlongated transparent bait container with hooks on the outside.

One type of early plug was later to be known as the "torpedo," a simple cigar shape with spinners. The "wigglers" had lips, collars or cutouts to provide extra action. The "torpedoes" were made in surface, near-surface and deep-running formats. For many years the basic Heddon seller was the "torpedo" with spinners and as many as five treble hooks.

Plugs with "built-in wiggle" during a steady retrieve were the forerunners of what would be called "crankbaits" half a century later. Some were capable of surface action and would wiggle when cranked under on a retrieve. As baitcasters, especially bass and pike casters, bought boxes of lures, each of the big bait companies developed a best lure of some sort and promoted it with national advertising. For many years there was a program of continual promotion for the old reliables, plus an almost annual introduction of new baits. The new lures were brought forth because the old ones had "already filled the tackle boxes" and couldn't maintain their sales records. This worked well for fishermen, for many of the trial lures became winners.

Typical long-time favorites include the Bass Oreno of South Bend, a wooden lure that floated until retrieved. Introduced about 1917, it made a very capable surface bait and was a wiggler on the way in. That, for example, was made in a wide variety of sizes with names such as Babe Oreno, Pike Oreno, Trout Oreno and so on, all of the same general design and action.

Creek Chub's leader was the Pikie Minnow with a metal lip. It also came in sizes for everything from panfish to offshore species. So did the Darter, possibly the most widely imitated wiggler of all. The Creek Chub Darter appeared about 1922-24, and was often called the "Two Thousand" for its catalog number.

Pflueger, a giant of the tackle industry, made everything the fisherman used and was into the field early with numerous plugs, including the metal-lipped Pal-O-Mine.

One of Shakespeare's early entries was an all-aluminum bait using spinners. The lure, whether you call it a plug or not, did not retain popularity.

Before we get into some baits that have come on since 1950 and appear to be revolutionary, let's make some general observations about fishing lures and the mysterious ways in which they come and go.

Forget the cute stories about lures that catch fishermen instead of fish, even though many of them have. There is an eerie reality in the ways certain baits achieve great popularity and then drop back into the pack or drift off into obscurity.

Although this happens in other kinds of fishing, it is the black bass that has spelled profit or loss for most lures of the past 100 years. This is partly because of the number of bass fishermen, but it is also a result of what seems to be a continual change in the actual appetites of the fish. Certain lures seem to "wear out" while others come on.

One explanation is that the fish that liked a certain bait have been

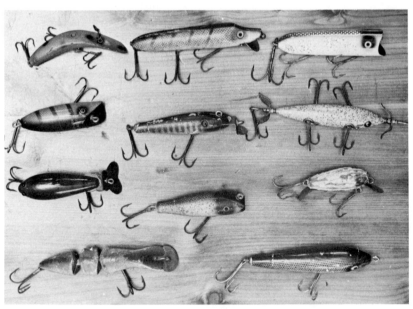

Middle-aged favorites of plug fishermen.
Top row, L. to R.: Flatfish, Heddon Vamp, Heddon Lucky 13.
Second row: South Bend Babe Oreno, Creek Chub Pikie,
Heddon Torpedo.
Third row: Creek Chub Crawdad, Creek Chub Darter, Tom Thumb.
Bottom: Heddon Game Fisher, Heddon Zaragossa.

caught. Another is that they have looked at it so long that they know it is a phony. The third suggestion is that bass have actually altered their appetites through months or years. In some cases, old-time baits, long discarded, have come on again to be popular.

At the same time, there undoubtedly have been good lures that never got off the ground because the maker could never get enough of them tried. It isn't that the fishermen wouldn't buy them and use them. They'd just never seen or heard of them. After bass tournaments became big news, lure popularity could come and go within days, whereas it may have taken a generation before.

In most cases the baits that boomed have had a new action and occasionally a completely new principle. One of the biggest sellers of all time has been the Helin Flatfish, which is simply a curved piece of wood, flattened at the front to produce a sort of searching wobble as it is retrieved.

The Helin Company has produced them in durable finishes, although the baits have never been particularly decorative. The hooking arrangement on Flatfish is unique, with small trebles mounted on outriggers. The instructions say to play fish gently so their efforts to escape will simply get them into more of the sharp little hooks. It works. The basic Flatfish is not intended for weedy waters and I believe most of its international success has been with trout and salmon, although it is a fine bass bait too. Imitations are endless.

The Flatfish didn't leap into prominence as quickly as those baits pushed into prominence by bass tournaments. Charles Helin invented it in 1933 and founded the Helin Tackle Company in 1937. In 1962, 29 years after the first Flatfish, he reported that enough had been sold to reach from Detroit to Miami if placed end to end. Charles Helin died in 1979, and in 1980 his son Wallace F. Helin reported that more than 50 million Flatfish had been sold. This, of course, does not include imitations.

Although the Flatfish is made in many sizes and some are intended for surface fishing, a large share of its popularity came from deep operation with a sinker ahead of the bait.

There has never been a poll, but I believe the Rapala, which began in Finland, is the most famous fishing lure ever used. America's craze came in 1962, almost 30 years after the first Rapala was made. The designer was a poor Finnish fisherman, Lauri Rapala. He began with a concept old to the lure business: gamefish strike those baitfish which behave differently from their fellows. Rapala was a troller, and if his bait had been promoted at the time of inception in 1936, it might not have gone over at all. The lures were too light to be cast with most tackle of that day. It took lighter equipment, especially spinning, to bring it into its own.

Rapala whittled the first plugs of pine bark, wrapping them in tinfoil; later the material was to be Ecuadorean balsa. The early baits worked for Rapala and his friends. Some were sent to America, but when Life Magazine ran a story on "The Lure Fish Can't Resist" in 1962, the Rapala took off. The lure was hard to make and cost much more than mass-produced baits, but fishermen clamored for it. For a time, premium prices were paid when supplies ran low.

American lure makers went to work immediately. So many look-alikes were made that I once ran an article with a single photo of a whole row of baits, all of which looked just alike. I was very cute about it. The caption read, *"Will the Real Rapala Please Stand Up?"*

This sounds like an indictment of the "counterfeit" Rapalas, which

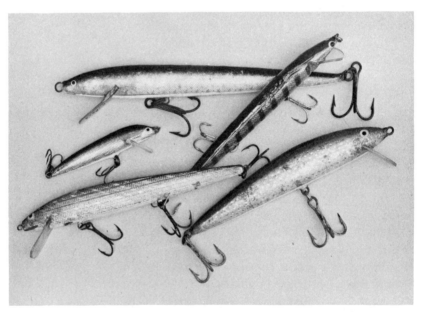

Rapala's design is one of the most imitated of all.
The "original" is hard to tell from the others.

appeared under other names. It's true that many of them did not have the action of the original and were made from completely different materials, but most of them were good baits and some were so near to the original that you had to look closely for a name.

Rapalas were soon made in a variety of sizes, some heavy enough for casting with plugging equipment. Balsa baits are fairly fragile and my first sample was crushed by a tarpon. The outstanding use for Rapalas seems to be with the smaller models, which can dance on the surface and then show a distinctive wobble when retrieved. By 1980, a great many plastic baits were made in the Rapala's silhouette. I believe only one firm was making them in balsa.

The Rapala millions produced a modern factory in Finland, but wealth meant very little to Lauri Rapala, poverty-stricken through most of his life. When he died in 1974 he had given away nearly all of his personal wealth. The Rapala success story is a combination of the right bait at the right time with the right scarcity and a name that appeals. Its manufacture in a distant country added to its attraction, but most important of all, it is a very, very good lure.

It would be nice to wrap up the plastic worm business with a dramatic appearance on a given date, but it didn't work that way. Soft lures of rubber and plastics have been around for a long time, generally with mediocre success. There were rubber worms, minnows and frogs in tackle catalogs back in the 1920s. Experimental "soft" baits have been around even longer.

The plastic worm is the most deadly artificial bass bait made, but it had trouble getting started. Not until about 1960 did it really begin to catch on.

Perhaps its ancestor was the eelskin used by surf fishermen and trollers as far back as the late 1800s or earlier. John Bickerdyke, in a book dedicated in 1885, refers to lures of "bacon skin," which handily translates to "porkrind." Long porkrinds had been used as "bobs."

In the 1950s there were some attempts at making worms of pork strips. They looked much the same as the later plastics, but had minor success. The first revolutionary plastic worms were fished almost entirely on the bottom in a technique that allowed bass to "chew on them for a while." Early worm fishermen used spinning tackle almost exclusively. Not until several years later was there wide use of other methods, including worms fished on the surface, at mid-depth and with fast retrieves. Before floating worms were designed, some careful operators managed to keep small "standard" worms suspended in the surface film.

The age of the worm began in the 1960s, and refinements in the 70s caused some good fishermen to become almost exclusively worm anglers. So effective had the bait become that it appeared the bass might have been designed for the worm instead of the other way around. When there was money on the table, as in the wildly proliferating bass tournaments, the worm brought big payoffs a large share of the time. There were hundreds of worm manufacturing concerns, and the question of faithful users wasn't "What lure?" but simply, "What color?"

An oddity of worm manufacture was the seeming love of black bass for exotic tastes, such as grape and licorice, which caused urchins to eat the merchandise in tackle stores. Options that work include "motor oil" and chartreuse, tastes and colors that seem to have few counterparts in nature.

Then there was the Big-O, a bass plug that sent manufacturers

*"Soft" baits were made in many forms after the
plastic worm became a success.*

hurtling for their drawing boards. For some reason it created a demand that has lasted for years, even though some of the offshoots of the original are very similar in both silhouette and action to baits made half a century before.

Not that the Big-O isn't a fine lure. It came in the approximate image of a shad and went with an extremely fast wiggle, almost a vibration. It appeared first as a winner in many big bass tourneys, carefully tuned and handmade. Competitors bought, borrowed and rented them, and manufacturers turned out imitations within days. The big blast was in 1973 when the species of bait was first called "fat plugs." Then the term "crankbait" took over, meaning a bait that was simply reeled or "cranked." The first users of the new lures cranked them fast, and there appeared some new casting reels that went faster than the traditional quadruple multiplying rigs. Later came stop-and-go retrieves and a variety of manipulations.

Of course these plugs were somewhat different than previous plugs, and that difference may have brought truly new fish-catching

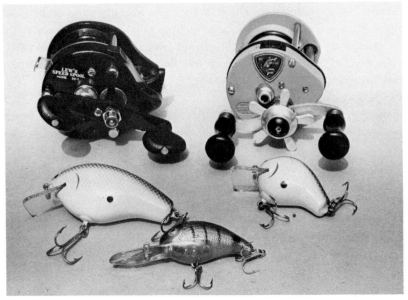

At first called "fat plugs," crankbaits maintained
a general appearance much like that of the original Big-O.
Reels in background are by Childre and Pflueger.

qualities. But the strangest thing about the new crankbaits' howling success is their remarkable similarity to earlier lures. Truly, it is the little things that count.

Of all the ancients that came forth in new garb, none was more redundant than the spinnerbait. It is simply a plastic skirt or similar attractor with one or more spinners (usually of spoon shape) riding above it on a wire outrigger. The spinnerbait was named rather gradually as it developed in several styles.

It wasn't called a "spinnerbait," but the old Shannon Twin Spinner of more than 50 years ago certainly fit the pattern. It was most popular as a big weighted bass fly with two small spoon-shaped spinners riding on equal-length outriggers above it. The hook turned up and, like the modern versions, it was quite weedless. There were bucktail versions in the same shape. Other less-known outrigger lures have also faded away.

Porkrind "wigglers" became popular in the 1920s. Best known at that time were Al Foss lures called the Shimmy, the Oriental, the Little Egypt and the Skidder. All of these involved husky spinners ahead of various small, weighted bodies. The Shimmy, one of the best of the lot, was usually used with a bucktail tied on a single hook with the porkrind attached to that. The first Foss patent was issued in 1916.

Somewhat later, the leader in the wigglers was the Fred Arbogast Company of Akron, Ohio. Theirs were the Hawaiian and the Sputterfuss.

Arbogast was a leader in plastic skirts for casting lures. Fred Arbogast started something considerably different, the Tin Liz, in the late 20s, apparently named after Henry Ford's product. It was a metal crippled minnow that lay on its side and employed a tail spinner. Later Arbogast leaders included the Jitterbug and the Hula Popper.

Shortly after World War II, a school of "clucker" fishermen came along, specializing in big surface spinners similar to those of the Arbogast Sputterfuss. This became pretty scientific business, the masters learning ways of tuning spinners for special effects. Most fishermen have at times sputtered a porkrind wiggler across the surface, although few are addicted to meticulous tuning.

Freshwater fishermen originated most of the light tackle and lures used at sea, but it may be that the jig, possibly the most ancient lure of all, traveled in the other direction. Ancient commercial fishermen "jigged" lures, baits and sometimes bare hooks nearly straight down from their boats and ships. Some saltwater casters used jigs and the similar "tin squid" long before the simple lures made their mark with light spinning gear.

The new school of jig anglers was mainly spinfishermen, and instead of confining jig operations to deep water they used a delicate touch and light lures (1/4 ounce was the most popular weight). Especially in salt water, they bumped the little feather, bucktail or nylon jig along the bottom to stir a tiny puff of mud or fine sand.

Many strikes were gentle, a fish nudging the lure or nipping it out of curiosity. Some of the real experts learned to play a coy tug-of-war with the fish, not setting the hook until after a half-dozen tugs when they felt he "really had it." As in many completely different kinds of fishing, this required true "fishing hands," gained by experience and concentration. Under other circumstances they might retrieve rapidly with bold sweeps of the rod and never lower the bait to the bottom.

Many jig anglers emerged, but Bill and Morrie Upperman of

The idea of the modern "spinnerbait" (right)
wasn't exactly new since spinners mounted on
outrigger weedguards appeared half a century
before on the Shannon Twin Spinner, (left).

Upperman Jigs were ringleaders, and one of the best was their friend, Phil Francis. Their deadliest operations were on the shallow flats, especially of the Florida Keys and the Caribbean. Some of the fish taken were of species not supposed to be catchable with artificials. Some anglers kept long "life lists" of species caught on jigs. One of the best known of the later jig experts was Alfred Reinfelder, a lure designer. His favorite, the *Baittail,* was a lead jig with a soft and flexible body of rubbery material rather than deer hair, feathers or nylon strands.

Inland fishermen were reluctant to use the word "jig" and tended to call their new lures by trade names. Extremely well known is the round-headed Doll Fly for panfish as well as impoundment bass and other deep-goers. The No-Alibi has a special reputation for southern crappie. The crappie fisherman, using spinning tackle, imitates the deep-jigging routine, tapping the bottom with his bait and then lifting it to let it fall back. For a time, fishermen in some areas called all jigs "No-Alibis."

The "Jig-n-Eel" is a combination of jig and pork eel (or whatever else might work) popular in impoundments, especially during cold weather when the bass are sluggish. Saltwater fishermen tend to "sweeten" their jigs with cut bait.

"Deep-jigging" may be a new term, but simple up-and-down jigging with a rod and reel is an old method. The typical deep-jigging rod is quite stiff with line that's a bit light to match it. Small line diameter is necessary in swift tidal currents to keep the jig from drifting off target, probably a wreck or rockpile.

Jigs catch almost anything.

CHAPTER SEVEN

THE FLIES

Fly fishing was old before other forms of artificial lures were seriously considered in sport angling. Until the torrent of literature on black bass appeared in the 1970s, more had been written about fly fishing than all other forms of angling put together.

Fly fishing had some early prestige that increased through the years. Walton was a bait soaker, but his co-author Cotton was strong on flies. You get the feeling that Cotton might have been less respectful of bait if it hadn't been for the presence of his revered associate.

By the early 17th century there were written testimonials to the superiority of fly angling over less aesthetic methods.

No other form of fishing has been so surrounded by ethics, "codes" and even formality. Fly fishing began as a trout method and that remains the backbone of its existence, but when it moved into other angling fields the tackle changed to fit the quarry, and the long rod now throws things that aren't "flies" at all. The streamer, of course, imitates baitfish instead of insects. Most Atlantic salmon wet "flies" are really lures and are fished in a way that has no relation to insects.

When you discuss fly fishing you are into all sorts of private preju-
dices that make it more fun. Some fishermen who do all their fishing
with fly rods will throw enormous popping bugs at saltwater billfish
or dredge the bottoms with leadcore lines, somewhat to the amaze-
ment of those who see that other tackle would often work better and
be much easier on the fisherman.

But, of course, the principle of sport fishing is the use of equipment
that handicaps the fisherman to some extent. No one denies that nets
or explosives are more efficient.

Within the loose trout and salmon fishing fraternity a variety of
cults exist. At one time the dry fly was considered the pinnacle of
scientific angling and the wet fly a coarser method. Then came the
term "nymph," which often means a simple wet fly. Some nymph
fishermen considered their art more advanced than dry fly fishing. A
few anglers will cast only to sighted or rising fish; others refuse to use
any weight on a fly or leader; some will use no fly involving bits of
cork or other rigged floatant; some insist on using nothing but standard and named patterns of flies. This last isn't much of a handicap
since there are multiple thousands of named flies and no one can list
them all.

Of "technical" waters beloved by modern fly fishermen,
Pennsylvania's Letort is near the ideal.

Eager searchers for perfection in imitation of natural insects are sometimes a bit let down when they probe reports from three centuries ago. They may have been a little short on Latin names but trout anglers of that time had already catalogued the hatches of flies on their favorite streams, sometimes being a bit too unyielding in setting dates for emergence of various species. The flies listed by Dame Juliana were firmly attached to the months of their appearances.

The entomology of 1500 A.D. might have been a bit primitive, but I am convinced that a careful angler of the year 2000 could hold his own using only the insect knowledge of that long gone year. True artists of fly presentation have proved repeatedly that a minimum of fly patterns and sizes can pass, even among selective trout.

This is not a detraction of entomologist-fishermen. I say without the slightest sour grapes that study of the insects and their relation to trout is as intriguing as study of the fish themselves. It is great to know what your fly represents, whether the trout knows or not. It's easy to get into the exact-imitation versus impression conflict, but it's unimportant. Those old timers may not have had chest waders or 7X monofilament leaders, but they could have walked up to the Yellow Breeches or the Battenkill and held their own, provided they were not distracted by the traffic.

Going into the personal lives of famous anglers isn't our game, but now and then one rates special attention if only because we wonder why he ever took up fishing for fun. Take Colonel Robert Venables, born in 1612 or 1613 in England. Because he was once locked up in the Tower of London for displeasing his boss, Oliver Cromwell, some have hinted he was less than a prospect for the Victoria Cross.

As I read it, Venables was a fighting so-and-so, and when Cromwell cashiered him for fouling up a West Indies campaign against the Spanish it would appear the colonel (then general) was in poor enough health to rate a furlough with pay instead of a cell near the Thames.

Venables fought with Parliament against the king, and later was sent to the islands with an ill-supplied army to face Spaniards, dysentery and starvation. He left his army there to make an unpopular report to his administration, and that was what took him to the Tower. When he was released he became a serious trout fisherman, knowing the game well enough to appear in an edition of Walton, who wrote flattering things about his skill.

*As new tackle and expertise developed,
fly fishermen regularly caught big trout that would
have been rare trophies with older gear.*

Venables was a fly angler with favorite rods of cane and blackthorn or crabtree sections and whalebone tips. Insisting that flies were the "most pleasant and delightful part of angling," he disagreed with the hard and fast rules demanding certain flies for certain months.

Said he, "When you come first to the river in the morning, with your rod beat upon the bushes or boughs which hang over the water. And by their falling upon the water you will see what sorts of flies are there in greatest numbers; if diverse sorts and equal in numbers, try them all, and you will quickly find which they most desire."

His work, *The Experienced Angler* (carrying an illustration of him in armor minus helmet) is dated 1662 in London. He goes into detail on construction of hair line, recommending slow twists. His methods of fly tying are fairly modern, although I don't know what sort of vise he used, if any. Most of his flyfishing advice is valid.

He advises fishing in swift streams on bright, calm days and explains that windy days will produce on the "plain deeps." He recommends large flies for muddy water and small ones for clear water. There's the familiar adage of dark flies for dark weather or dark waters and a recommendation that "for every sort of fly have three; one of a lighter color, another sadder than the natural fly, and a third of the exact color with the fly, to suit all waters and weathers as before." He recommends wetting any fly to view its true color and that special attention be given to the belly of the fly, since that's what the fish sees most.

Trout seekers who have been frustrated in slow limestone streams or clear sloughs will nod agreement to Venables' explanation that fish living in slow, sluggish waters move slowly, see the fly plainly and are hard to fool.

He said that a fly fisherman can handle a line twice the length of his rod, but doesn't tell us how to land a fish with such gear. We assume no reel was involved, but like Cotton, he may have had a gillie.

Some of the most famous fishermen are noted for their philosophy more than the length of their casts or fineness of their tippets. The history of angling literature is a special route, but I think we should mention Alfred Ronalds, who came forth with *The Fly Fisher's Entomology* in 1836. His work showed drawings of 47 natural flies and the counterfeits to match them. Then he planted a milestone by giving scientific definitions of the flies as well as their common names. Later experts have found some fallacies and certainly broadened the field, but anyone memorizing his work of almost 150 years ago could dazzle 99 percent of today's trout fishermen.

During the 19th century in America, those who used fly tackle for other fishes weren't nearly as literary as trout anglers. For example, in the 20th century Harold Gibbs of Rhode Island designed the Gibbs Striper, an excellent striped bass streamer. He is recognized as the father of fly rod striper fishing. Of course Gibbs, top-notch angler, was a starter of the modern striper-on-the-fly business. But you'll find casual mention of striper fishing with fly rods much earlier, so Gibbs wasn't the very first. The "very first" at anything is hard to pin down.

Mary Orvis Marbury, daughter of Charles F. Orvis, produced *Favorite Flies and their Histories* in 1892. While it may not compete favorably with later works on entomology, it certainly is unique for its time. It includes a practical treatise on fly classification.

A fly's "history" is likely to be disappointing in one respect. Whereas historians are likely to set down a definite date for invention of the light bulb or printing press, even a well-known fly usually

Big two-handed salmon rod fitted with Malloch reel
was an aristocratic combination almost a century ago.
(Photo by George Anderson)

appears on the scene less abruptly. Remember that it may take years for it to achieve any general popularity, and perhaps it may go nameless for some time. The "inventor" may have done little more than give it an appealing name. "Little brown fuzzy thing" or "big red thing with white wings" may serve for a time, but identification among several thousand flies demands more precise nomenclature.

Favorite Flies employs a form used much later by Joe Bates in his streamer book. He might have done the job the hard way, but it's difficult to personalize things any better. In *Favorite Flies* 300 patterns are discussed in letters from well-known fishermen in all parts of the country.

In some cases the correspondent may have originated one of the flies himself, but in most instances he simply tells how he used a given pattern or patterns. These writers also tended to wander into other fishing experiences that were just as informative as the original subject—or more so.

Edward K. Landis, hardly a purist, whatever his expertise, tells how he found it impossible to catch any bass on the flies he was using. He finally attached a small, brown, live toad to a large brown hackle with exemplary success. After that, he said, when fly fishing was slow he always hunted toads.

Another of the experts recommends foregoing flies if they simply won't work for trout, and explains how worms can be kept hale and hearty in the damp recesses of a leader box.

It's surprising that the writings of Henry Guy Carlton show so seldom in fishing history. The man seemed to have more humor than any of the better known authors. Perhaps his obscurity among anglers is simply because he wasn't noted for writing fishing books, but some of his essays certainly surpass the stiff humor in most angling literature. Of flies in general, he was quoted in the Marbury book:

> "The artificial fly is a fish-hook to which variously colored feathers have been tied, and is supposed to be easily mistaken by a fish for a real fly. If this be true, it is a strong proof that a fish hasn't sense enough to come in when it rains, and doesn't deserve to live. . . .
>
> "Artificial flies are all named. There are the 'Professor,' the 'Hackle,' the 'Ibis,' the 'Yellow Sally,' and several other breeds.

Whenever a bilious angler has no luck, and nothing to do, he sits down and concocts a new swindle in feathers, and christens it with a nine-jointed Indian name, and at once every angler in the country rushes in and pays $2 a dozen for samples."

A non-fly fisherman would probably describe the hackle flies as fuzzy ones without wings. Evidently the first known fly pattern was the Red Hackle. The fly, described by Aelian as used by the Macedonians in the 3rd century after Christ, was made of red wool and employed wax-colored feathers from under a cock's wattles. I doubt if that fly was truly a Red Hackle, but it had the right color.

One of Dame Juliana's flies is described as follows:

"In the begynning of Maye a good flye, the body of roddyd wull and lappid abowte wyth blacke silke; the wynges of the drake of the redde capons hakyll."

Close enough, I guess. Anyway, the hackle flies have worked ever since.

The Coachman flies, like many others, cling to an appealing name while taking all sorts of offshoots from the original. The Royal Coachman is a dressed-up version of the first models. The Marbury book quotes David Foster in his book, *Scientific Angler,* on the origin of the Coachman flies:

"A thorough command of the rod and line is as essential and important as the wielding of the whip in the case of the tandem or four-in-hand drive. We are reminded of this analogy that the most skillful cast we ever knew wielded the whip. We refer to the famous coachman, Tom Bosworth.

"Old Tom had, in the early part of his life, driven three successive British sovereigns, namely the Fourth George, the Fourth William, and finally, for a lengthened period, Her Majesty Queen Victoria. As a successful fisherman, old Tom, when known to the writer, was unsurpassed. . . . A favorite freak of his with the whip was to take the pipe from the teeth of a passing pedestrian by a calculated whirl of the whip, and his aptitude was as remarkably exemplified for a limited distance in the use of the rod. Bosworth originated the Coachman fly so much appreciated for night fishing. This artificial has recently been much used as a fancy fly for day fishing, and with considerable success."

We can jump to 1970 for another demonstration of the whip expert in fly fishing. When Hugh Peltz, prominent quarter-horse fancier and rancher, undertook distance fly casting, his range was immediately spectacular. Since he claimed little flyfishing experience, veteran fly casters were amazed. Peltz finally explained the phenomenon. He had driven strings of pack mules years earlier and motions with the long whip, he said, "were just like those with a fly rod."

Angling literature in America has invariably centered about the East. Clear into the 1950s Eastern writers wrote of their Western trout adventures as if they had daringly penetrated the wilds in the name of sport. They were a little late, for Pacific coast trout fishing had been going on since 1876. One of the famous Western fishing clubs, the McCloud River Club, began in 1878, while the Golden Gate Angling and Casting Club and the San Francisco Fly Casting Club came along in 1893. Yellowstone Park fishing had received rave notices by 1870.

It was around that time that the Western species of trout were on their way to streams all over the world. For example, Colorado's Gunnison had good rainbow trout fishing by 1890, the trout having

Among the bass bugs of the 1930s were the Dragon Fly,
Hair Mouse and Stunted Skunk.
The reel is a Zwarg, successor to the vom Hofe.

been brought from farther west. There had been little done with
Pacific salmon on flies, but steelhead attracted fishermen in the
1870s. Rudyard Kipling told of steelhead fishing in 1889 on the Clack-
amas River in Oregon. By 1930 it was frequently reported that the
West Coast steelhead streams were overcrowded.

Any salmon fisherman was equipped for a few black bass now and
then, geography permitting, and the early bass flies of the 19th century were generally outsized models of brighter wet flies for trout. In
some early catalogs, the "lake flies" and "bass flies" were combined
in one listing. Trolling flies from a canoe is a time-honored method
for landlocked salmon. Perhaps "lake flies" were for big trout or for
salmon.

Flies had been fished on the surface and just beneath it for a long
while before the time of Theodore Gordon, generally recognized as
America's father of the dry fly. Gordon, born in 1854, was something
special. Evidently a victim of tuberculosis, he lived much of his life in
retirement on the Neversink in the New York Catskills. He had used
what might be called a pseudo-dry fly, drying wet flies with false
casting and then floating them briefly with an upstream cast. He
corresponded with Frederic Halford, the English angler-author and
dry fly expert, about 1890 and eventually tied stiff-hackle flies that rode
high on water that was faster than Halford usually fished. The Quill
Gordon, one of America's most famous flies, was his creation. Like
most famous flies, it has so many variations due to varied materials
and individual whims that some models are unrecognizable, but the
name has held. The small dry fly was dependent upon metallurgy,
working well only with light hooks.

Historical flies often cling to their names after losing almost all
other identity. I am awed by the modern variations of Lefty's Deceiver,
an excellent saltwater (and freshwater too, for that matter) streamer,
originated by Lefty Kreh a few years ago. No matter how good a
fisherman Lefty Kreh is, or how fine the original streamer is, it's
the name that intrigues happy tiers who use it for things that Kreh
wouldn't recognize, and might scare him.

There is more to be said about Halford (Mr. Dry Fly) and G.E.M.
Skues (Mister Nymph), but let's check developments rather than
literature. Fly fishing for trout was so swathed in tradition in Britain
that when Skues favored nymphs or wets for certain conditions he set
off a long and rather stuffy argument between dry fly purists and

those who used nymphs, never mind how much skill was involved. After Gordon floated the dry fly, American trout fishermen remained democratic and used what they liked best. However, until about 1955 (I have to pick a date, even if it's a rough one) there had been a feeling that wet flies were less sophisticated than drys. Then, when the term "nymph" became more popular, nymph fishermen were honored and "wet" fishermen were scorned, none of which meant a great deal to the trout. Temporarily, you could gain respect by cutting the wings off your wets. Finally, for heaven's sake, it was ethical to put sinkers on them.

Before the dry fly had become established there had been considerable British discussion as to whether a fly should be fished upstream or down. This went on for thousands of pages in rather heated discourses. There were a few unsung moderates who did it either way as conditions seemed to call for it. In America, the matter was never considered an international emergency.

Fly fishermen have been the leaders in wade fishing. Development

Peckinpaugh's "Night Bug" developed in many directions.
The three lower bugs are similar to the original
"Feather Minnow." The large white popper was designed
for sailfish.

of waterproof "wading stockings" (hip boots) and "wading trousers" isn't very well recorded in fishing literature, although they were advertised in American catalogs before 1880. There was and is less wading in Britain, largely because the streams there are more likely to have cleared banks, and because truly mountainous country makes wading more important.

Anglers of other countries sometimes poke a little fun at the American's addiction to getting into the water. I once talked with an Englishman who had fished over much of the world. He said, "I have been to the Rocky Mountains where the Americans wade right up the middle of the bloody rivers!"

Through the past 100 years and more, one of the chief problems of the stream fisherman has been finding waders that don't leak. Although wading problems are not conducive to the literary flights that attend fly patterns and fly rod construction, they cause me to search for mentions in old writings.

William Scrope, the English author who specialized in salmon fishing, had a bit of startling advice for waders of the mid-1800s before wading "trousers" or "stockings" were commonly used. He said that those who were delicate and waded in February when it freezes should pull down their stockings at intervals to examine their legs. If they were black or purple, he said, it would be best to head for dry land, but added that if they were only rubicund (reddish) there was nothing to worry about.

Scrope also said you should go no deeper than the fifth button of your waistcoat. He made no reference to tee shirts or fishing vests. The vest may have developed gradually as special pockets appeared on an assortment of shirts and coats. However, Lee Wulff, the 20th century master, is generally credited with introduction of the finished article.

The British have known a great deal about trout for 400 years. Their 19th century writers covered the essentials so thoroughly that even advanced science can add little to their knowledge of trout and salmon vision, locomotion and general habits. With revision for characteristics of the species found only in America, their information pretty well covers the field. For example, there are accounts of tagging operations back in Walton's time. The French, leading scientists of the last century, never seemed to go so deeply into fly fishing, or at least didn't say very much about it.

Nobody but the Americans, however, seemed to use flies to catch new fish species. Although the British hunted tigers in India and elephants in Africa, they tended to reserve their flies for trout and Atlantic salmon. Once the Yanks started throwing flies, they showed them to everything from alligators to tuna.

Bass fishermen used flies shaped like wet trout flies, although larger. Floating flies were also used now and then for bass, particularly smallmouths, but their big scene came with the bass bug.

Ernest H. Peckinpaugh of Chattanooga, Tennessee, is credited as originator of the modern bass bug. A.J. McClane in his *Fishing Encyclopedia* quotes Peckinpaugh as saying he had noted a bucktail on the surface was best at times for bluegills, and so he worked up bugs on double hooks (so the cork body could be secured better). It was about 1910 or 1911, Peckinpaugh said, that he made some larger ones for night fishing for bass and called them Night Bugs.

From then on bass bugs took endless forms. Will H. Dilg publicized the cork-bodied bugs, and Peckinpaugh credited him with much of their popularity. Balsa has been used instead of cork on many models, and plastic has worked well. It was long after their origin that descriptive names accurately separated the types. The "popping bug" has a flat or concave nose for maximum noise, the "slider" began as a "feather minnow" and has a bullet-shaped head for less raucous operation. The "hair bug," "powderpuff" or "hair mouse" are all the same thing, tied with the hair (usually deer hair) installed so that the ends are out in a "burr" silhouette.

A highly popular fly rod lure of the 1920s, the Tuttle's Devil Bug, was a modification of the hair bug in which much of the hair was tied down to form a fairly solid body. It remains a much-used design. There have been legions of hair mice, some complete with beady eyes and leather tails. For the most part, full-size bass bugs require fairly powerful rods, although many hair models with large silhouettes can be thrown with light equipment of trout specifications.

When the fly rod really went to sea after World War II, some of the more powerful models were used to cast monstrous Styrofoam "sailfish bugs," larger than any true insect and imitating something entirely different. In any event, the general term of "bass bug" can't quite cover the saltwater designs.

Small fly rod spoons, little wooden plugs and spinner-fly combinations burdened bass rods unmercifully until the advent of spinning.

Light tackle craze of the post-war era was the bonefish.
Although fly gear had been used on them much earlier,
it was the 1950s before bonefishing with flies
became widespread.

Most of them were miniatures of successful baitcasting and trolling lures. They were cast short and sloppily, but they filled the gap when bass weren't striking on the surface. Of the hundreds of designs of spinners and spoons, we might mention the Pflueger Luminous Tandem Spinner as at least somewhat unique. At one time it was feared luminous baits would deplete the rivers, lakes and seas. The same thing happened when the first fluorescent flies appeared much later.

Although I complain about their terrible casting qualities on a fly rod, tandem spinners were a favorite of my youth. You false-casted some line, allowed the spinner to plunk in and reach the desired depth, and then stripped it back to near the rod tip. Maybe it wasn't really fly fishing but we used fly rods. Spinning tackle mercifully took over the little wood and metal lures, a relief to aching wrists.

Rods were something of a handicap in early saltwater fly fishing. A two-handed salmon rod used on tarpon was likely to be 12 feet long, and when a 6-inch chicken-feather streamer was attached it became an awesome tool. The first saltwater rod I owned was only 9½ feet long, of bamboo. Intended for one hand, it weighed 8½ ounces. After about 1955 only a very few traditionalists used bamboo rods in salt water, glass being lighter and less expensive. Graphite also joined in.

Fly fishing for saltwater fish never really became popular until after World War II, but there were some individuals who did it 50 years before that. Around the turn of the century the few fly casters caught "baby" tarpon, weakfish and striped bass on flies regularly. Not everyone shrank from the giants.

Half a century later when tarpon fly fishermen were congratulating themselves on occasional catches of fish near 100 pounds, some of them were a bit abashed when handed *Book of the Tarpon* by A.W. Dimock. Dimock was hooking and fighting big tarpon along Florida's southwest coast with ordinary fly rods about the turn of the century. He landed his silver kings by rolling them into a canoe along with a little sea water. His brother took pictures of it.

Heavy-duty fly fishing became tougher and tougher when everybody tried to use bigger and bigger streamers. It was a strain on roosters, rods and arms. Somewhere about 1966 fly tiers began to learn ways of giving a long silhouette without too many feathers. Some perceptive tarpon fishermen began to note that some of the slightly smaller streamers were just as good or better than the big ones, sank faster when necessary, and cast easily. The offshore fishermen continued to use big streamers and bugs, but they were getting their fish within range with teasers and chum lines, which involved less casting.

While more powerful rods of lighter weight handled bigger lures with less effort, the other end of fly fishing—the delicate part—advanced too. Lighter glass and graphite rods were preferred by some fishermen, but monofilament leader material, which finally superseded horsehair and silkworm gut, had more effect on actual presentation. With monofilament, it was possible to use a 6X or 7X leader (.004 inch diameter) on selective trout and still retain enough strength to have a chance at landing good-sized fish.

Tiny leader diameter made tiny flies more practical. Insects that had to be ignored by earlier fishermen could now be matched. Whereas a

As rods became more powerful and were matched
by new lines, fly fishermen began to use big streamers
like these in salt water.

No. 14 fly was once considered small, the delicate nylon monofilament leaders could handle flies into the 20s for those skillful enough to cast them and bright-eyed enough to watch them. Only a few diehards stayed long with gut leaders after monofilament appeared.

Along with the monofilament leaders, new fly line materials came after World War II, and silk lines lost their popularity. The new materials didn't require much care, dressing or cleaning.

Then monofilament did something special for fly fishing beginning in 1946, and it didn't involve leaders. Two tournament casters, Phillip C. Miraville and Jim Green of San Francisco's Golden Gate Casting Club, introduced monofilament running line to be attached to "shooting heads." Until monofilament, the running line was of silk. When Green won the distance fly event with monofilament at the next national tournament, his fly went 149 feet.

After its success on the tournament platform, monofilament running line was adopted by a variety of fishermen, especially West Coast steelheaders. With it a fisherman could not only cast great distance, he could get a "sinking head" down deep in a hurry.

The dry and wet patterns for trout had been around for centuries before streamers began to be popular. Nobody can say at just what point an ordinary wet fly leaves off and a streamer begins. Make the "wet" Royal Coachman a little long in the body and wing and call it a streamer. Streamers are usually moved like swimming baitfish but they can be dead-drifted too. The simplest way of describing a streamer is to say that it represents a small fish, whereas a "wet" or "dry" trout fly represents an insect. The fish have not really clarified it for us so let's leave it at that.

I believe streamers really became popular in the 1920s, but we learn that Theodore Gordon, the dry fly "father," tied a streamer called the Bumblepuppy as far back as 1880. Gordon, best known for his trout fishing, took striped bass on his streamer as well as other species. But like most patterns its specifications are vague, and it is apparent that Gordon used the term loosely for a number of streamer-type flies.

My streamer bible is *Streamers & Bucktails, the Big Fish Flies* by Joseph D. Bates, Jr. He researched all of the popular patterns and some you never heard of, put them all in one big volume, giving the exact or approximate dates of origin for many of the most popular ones. Although he digs into some ancient fly patterns with his usual meticulous detail, the streamer conversion dates tend to be after 1920. What happened was that many tiers took long-successful attractor fly patterns and converted them into streamers. That is, the basic colors, and often the materials, were about the same with the silhouettes lengthened.

Sometimes "bucktails" are listed separately from feather streamers, but they're all streamers in silhouette and fishing method. A few things were a mite revolutionary, however. One winner is the Muddler Minnow, a burr-headed creation of Don Gapen around 1950. It comes close to an underwater imitation of the sculpin and its relatives, all favorite trout foods. Floated on the surface it was a pretty good grasshopper. The general design was spliced into many other streamers of varied colors, and most were winners on trout and black bass. They also work in salt water but never have become very popular there. I have heard the No. 10 white Muddler called the best all-around trout fly ever designed. Maybe so.

Combinations of new tackle and techniques took the fly to new

*In the late twentieth century, fly fishing for
trout went to the extremes with giant
Muddler Minnow and tiny dry fly being cast
for the same fish.*

depths, beginning about 1950. The shooting head in a variety of weights was advertised as "slow-sinking," "medium-sinking" and "fast-sinking" in the 1970s. By the 80s there were heads that acquired descriptive terms such as "Cannonball." What you had was 25 or 30 feet of sinker that could be false-casted.

One of the first inroads of the sinking heads had been in steelhead fishing. This was completely different from a simple wet fly with a little lead wire wrapped around the body. The whole works sank, giving the bottom-bumping fly much more appeal by keeping it near bottom where the fish were, especially on rivers where steelhead were noted for keeping their stomachs near the gravel. The flies could be cast a little upstream and "dead-drifted," much as the Cherry Bobber, a casting tackle breakthrough, had been handled. Since the bigger steelhead tend to stay deep, this rewrote the record books pretty rapidly.

What did the bottom flies represent? Well, some of them were simple baits of fluorescent yarn that were thought to approach the appearance of salmon eggs, which steelhead dearly love. One steelhead expert pronounced that one of his fly patterns was intended to look like a Cherry Bobber.

That steelheader's explanation is a succinct way of showing that the flyfishing purist was using new gear to compete with spinning and casting tackle on its own ground. The sinking head went to salt water for a number of reef fish that had never been shown flies before, and even came to the black bass lakes to display some rather long and wriggly streamers that competed with plastic worms.

There was a flyfishing boom late in the 1970s, spiced by more efficient tackle and augmented by a new flood of literature and fly-fishing schools.

CHAPTER EIGHT

THE SALT

They lashed themselves to the rails of plunging sailing ships and jigged handlines for cod off Newfoundland, victims of exposure and disease a long way from their European homes. They rowed into deadly banks of swirling fog in tiny dories, and when fish and politics mixed they did their cold, wet work under the muzzles of protective warships.

It is no wonder that it was a long time before anyone seriously considered fishing in the sea for fun. Oh, the Pilgrims enjoyed a little trolling for bluefish, and now and then some wandering salmon angler cast a fly for a striped bass or some other ocean fish that happened to be within range. But sport fishing at sea lacked tradition, and there was no appropriate tackle, no appropriate boats and hardly any knowledge of what lived in the oceans. There was little record of oceanic fish movements.

Striped bass clubs of the New England coast probably started serious coastal sport fishing in America. Business tycoons engaged in saltwater sport fishing gave the game dignity and respect.

The industrialists who founded the clubs used a variety of rod materials, but didn't make their rods very long. In time, the Henshall "black bass rod" became highly popular for inland fishing and must have influenced striper rods, even though they were somewhat heavier. The Henshall rod was for baitcasting (natural baits) and was quite different from the early Kentucky rods, considerably shorter and made to balance like an "American trout rod." The trout rod of that time was a fly rod, of course, but its balance for other purposes was deemed ideal by Henshall and his followers.

The striper clubs did things in a big way. There was some true ground-based surf casting, but their best known efforts involved throwing from stands built along the rocky New England shores. They had professional chummers and gaffers, plush clubhouses and carrier pigeons for business purposes. They sold their catch, but that certainly didn't cover expenses.

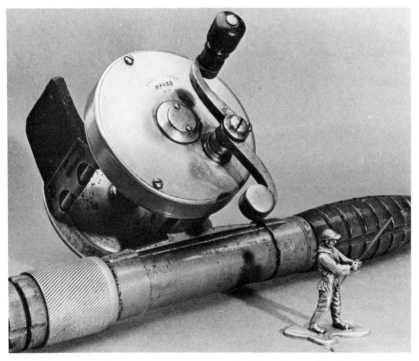

Thomas J. Conroy heavy-duty reel of the "knuckle-buster" type that was used on striped bass and other saltwater fish before invention of the star drag.

They developed into some of the finest casters of large baits, using reels, later to be known as "knucklebusters," without drags. When the fish went, the handle turned, and a 50-pound striper whirled it with authority. They learned spot casting to sighted swirls made by striped bass in a wild surf, or they might get a flashing glimpse of the fish itself. Even though chummers and gaffers were present and the platforms sturdy, it was no sissy sport, and there were occasions when ardent sportsmen disappeared under green water.

Thumbstalls were made of rubber or leather. In later years many were made of elastic cloth with leather facing. Some stand casters wore cots on both hands since they had learned to cast from either right or left side. Fish could appear anywhere in front of the stand, no matter how carefully the chum was fed.

Vom Hofe reels were some of the first to venture into offshore big game fishing. The one at left, without a star drag, was patented in 1896.
The reel with star drag (a major breakthrough) was patented in 1902.

Although a variety of baits was used, menhaden was a favorite when available. Evidently artificials weren't used much, if at all, even though there had been some fly fishing for striped bass much earlier.

How far could the stand fisherman cast? They did not use the extremely long rods of later surf anglers, and some stories of their prowess seem a bit over-enthusiastic. I'm inclined to doubt accounts of throws of "well over 100 yards," but none of us was there.

Most of the club members were from New York, but one association, the Providence Club, was made up mainly of Rhode Islanders. Some other clubs were Squibnocket, Cuttyhunk, Pasque Island, West Island and Cohasset Narrows. Membership was expensive, and in this case at least, the "rockfish" was rather exclusive, an aristocrat to compete with the Atlantic salmon.

The stands were usually mounted on pipes sunk in holes drilled in shoreline stone. Most could be taken down during the off season. They were set above high tide mark, giving a caster considerable height advantage, even though waves sometimes broke over them.

The striped bass left the New England coast unaccountably about 1900, not to return in numbers for more than 30 years. Only empty stone sockets that held the steel pipes now show where the stands were.

The first saltwater sport fishing was at the very edge of the sea. It took a very rich man to go far from shore to catch fish for fun, and it was almost 1800 before that happened. In the meantime, some startling rumors circulated about the Florida tarpon, said to be a fish no sporting tackle could hold. So although it was in the Pacific that offshore angling really began, it was the Atlantic tarpon that stirred enthusiasm for giant fish on light gear. In the late 1800s you could row a skiff to acres of rolling tarpon from any of 100 points in Florida.

In one respect the tarpon is a fake. No other fish begins a fight with so wild a twisting leap. A man looking upward to 100 pounds of writhing silver and great saucer eyes is likely to feel such a fury could never be landed on sporting tackle.

Many years passed before fishermen learned that, although the tarpon is a great leaper and explosive striker, it can actually be handled with light gear in reasonably shallow water once the initial gyrations have subsided. In the meantime, anglers tried heavier and heavier tackle. At first, such a fish seemed a poor target for finesse.

In the case of the tarpon, use of a spear was not considered unsporting. And the silver king was a good spear target because of its habit of rolling. A few fly fishermen caught small ones on flies, but fish over 75 pounds were subjects of awe. Few outfits were considered capable of handling tarpon and some of the recommended tackle was awesome, being quite similar to what was later used for sharks.

A Florida trek became stylish for daring anglers wanting to match wits and muscle with tarpon. One sportsman offered to pay the expenses of anyone who could land a large specimen. The jinx was broken in 1885 when William H. Wood caught a tarpon weighing 93 pounds. The methods advocated by Wood were similar to those of some later fishermen who used bait and allowed the fish to swallow it. A big bait, usually a dead mullet, is still fished on the bottom with slack line. Actually, it is a form of gorge fishing, even though a hook is used. This method is no longer considered very sporting, but it's certainly efficient.

Apparently patience was a main feature of Wood's method. Other fishermen had tried to set large hooks into the tarpon's bony jaws as soon as the fish struck, only to see the bait thrown back in their faces.

Plug casters stake out at the mouth of a tidal river
to cast for big tarpon. Light-tackle plugging
came into its own in the 50s and 60s.

126

Henry Guy Carlton gave his version of the method:

"The best bait for tarpon is half a mullet, tied on to the hook with a string. The fisherman may sometimes prefer other bait, which is just as effective on days when the tarpon are not biting.

"The tarpon bites by taking the bait into his mouth. This theory is not disputed by advanced naturalists. He then swallows it, closes his eyes for a few moments in meditation, and proceeds to move off. At this juncture the careful angler will wake up.

"To strike the tarpon properly, wait until he has proceeded about 50 feet, when, raising the rod and tightening the line, a strong, triple yank will set the hook firmly, and the tarpon will show his sudden interest by a jump of 7 feet for fresh air. At this moment a kick and a few well-chosen words will arouse the nigger, who will weigh anchor. The anchor must be weighed at once or the tarpon will never be.

"A tarpon's first desire, on finding that his hunk of mullet contains a gift with a string tied to it, is to bite a hole in the sky, and then to visit Brazil or Iceland and arrive that day. This excursion must be promptly discouraged by pressure on the line and an industrious combination of nigger and oars, or the angler will lose fish and salvation simultaneously.

"Failing to reach Queenstown or Rio Janeiro, the tarpon again takes a hurried view of the scenery and starts for Aspinwall, changes his mind, throws four hand springs, heads for New Orleans, exhibits himself once more in mid-air, makes a break for Havana, and then, getting warmed up, proceeds to show what he can really do. A bewildering series of complicated evolutions follows for two hours, at the end of which time he is alongside, and the nigger skillfully knocks him off the hook with the gaff, and the proud and happy angler returns to the hotel to cuss."

Carlton fished Jupiter Inlet.

When William C. Harris described tarpon tackle in *The American Angler* in 1895 he recommended a good striped bass reel with a leather guard for thumb protection and 500 to 600 feet of Cuttyhunk linen line. The rod would be short and stiff, from 6 to 7 feet long. The hook was a 10/0 O'Shaughnessy with a 3-foot soft-linen or cotton snell about the diameter of a lead pencil. About that time vom Hofe made a reel called the "Silver King." It was used with a 7-foot Thomas J. Conroy rod by H.C. Harmsworth, a prominent British sportsman who pursued tarpon with success.

After Wood caught his big fish there was a storm of claims, and since there was no official record keeping at the time, tarpon fishing history becomes incomplete. It was only a few years before A.W. Dimock wrote of his adventures with fly rods and canoes in tarpon country.

Dimock cruised inshore Florida with a live-aboard cruiser and did things with rod and reel that were considered revolutionary when repeated 50 years later. His brother photographed much of it, producing some of the best action photographs of tarpon ever seen, including sequences in which fisherman, tarpon and canoe are equally half-submerged. This occurred around 1900 and shortly afterward. There were several such Florida trips.

For more than 80 years, Boca Grande Pass of the Gulf Coast has been a center for tarpon fishing, generally over fairly deep water, quite different from that of the Florida Keys flats or the Florida back country.

Mary A. Mitchell, writing in *Antique Angler,* tells how tarpon fishing went formal. She explains that in the 1890s, Useppa Island, located in Boca Grande Pass, was acquired by John Roach of Chicago as a home site. Later, he erected an inn and during the best tarpon season (May through July) his steam yacht would tow anglers in rowboats out to tarpon water where they could fish individually. Barron Collier, leader in development of south Florida, bought the island in 1910 and established the Izaak Walton Tarpon Club. Members commemorated their catches with appropriate buttons, much like those used by tuna club anglers of California.

Boca Grande has continued as a tarpon center and has offered a unique approach to big game fishermen. Shore is only a few moments from the trolling, casting or drifting grounds. The open inboard "tarpon boat" was at least partly developed there, a comfortable craft with uncluttered cockpit intended for short hauls. Tarpon fishing certainly became civilized.

A tarpon fishery that has waxed and waned during the past 40 years is near Homosassa and Crystal River, Florida, where the fish are of

*Dr. Charles F. Holder and his 183-pound tuna taken in
1898, the first large tuna ever to be taken on rod and reel.
It was this catch, and Dr. Holder's enthusiasm,
that led to the formation of the Tuna Club at Avalon,
Santa Catalina, CA.
(Photo from the Joe Brooks Collection, property of the IGFA)*

especially blocky build. It is now the most popular scene for fly rodders seeking records. No one has explained why the Homosassa fish are so heavy or where they come from.

While the tarpon was responsible for a sudden spurt in inshore fishing, it was the Pacific tuna that moved sportsmen into deep water. Charles Frederick Holder led the way when he caught a 183-pound tuna off Catalina Island in 1898, an event that competed with the Spanish-American War for public interest. Apparently other tuna had been caught on rod and reel but Holder was the right man at the right time, for he was well known as a newspaper and magazine editor (*Los Angeles Tribune* and *California Illustrated*) and author of a book on biology.

The Holder tuna catch must have been quite a fray. It took 3 hours and 45 minutes, and at one time the boat capsized. Holder and his guide, Jim Gardner, got back aboard and took up where they had left off.

By that time most of the basics of deep-water fishing were available. The reels had both mechanical drags and leather thumbing gadgets. The drags weren't good enough to stand on their own but were being improved rapidly.

To become a member of the Catalina Tuna Club you had to catch a tuna weighing at least 100 pounds on rod and reel with line no heavier than 24-thread (72-pound-test). You received a button when you caught your fish—and organized competition moved into salt water. It was a game of rich men, and it didn't take long for them to learn of it. They came from around the world and schemed for big fish in far places. Remember, the offshore sportfishing boat hadn't existed except as a conversion of something else. Outriggers, fighting chairs and electronics were yet to come.

Zane Grey did more to promote deep-water fishing than any other man, but he was a thorn in the side of less flamboyant anglers who snickered at his colorful accounts of fishing adventures and groaned when he complained of angling rules. For example, Grey insisted that landing a fish with a broken rod or with a rod substituted for a broken one was more difficult than landing the same fish if all went well. Therefore, he said, such a catch should be allowed in the record books.

From Grey's viewpoint big-game fishing was adventure—sweating, muscle-straining adventure that took the angler into the unknown. He didn't know what monsters awaited him.

Grey soaked his hands in brine and practiced fish playing for hours on land, using big rods and lines. He had just traced the bloody adventures of gunfighters across the Western plains and was in no mood for too much regulation in his fishing, and that's what finally caused some trouble. Already successful as an author, he was willing to spend large sums on boats and skippers when he began making his summer headquarters at the Catalina Tuna Club in 1915. Billfish were his passion and he tried to turn the Catalina club toward them.

Grey tended to belittle the catches of some of the other members. W.C. Boschen, a highly experienced deep-water fisherman, caught a broadbill that weighed 463 pounds in 1917. Grey didn't think that was such a big deal because the fish had been hooked "in the heart." This did little to cement his friendship with Boschen. Grey landed a 418-pound broadbill himself in 1920. His lurid stories of that catch were a bit rich for some of his associates who had never considered fishing to be a life and death matter.

*After World War II the charter boat opened offshore
fishing to hosts of anglers. Here a mate lands
a Gulf Stream sailfish in the 1950s.*

A quote from Grey's story of one of his swordfish battles shows the colorful language that brought laughs from fishermen who had been reading accounts of World War I. He said:

".... Why did I keep it up? I could not give up and I concluded I was crazy . . . I sweat, I panted, I whistled, I bled—and my arms were dead, and my hands raw and my heart seemed about to burst."

But it was a lady who finally caused Grey to part with the Catalina club. She was slight-of-build Mrs. Keith Spalding, who landed a 426-pound broadbill in 1921. Her exploit made the muscle-bulging efforts of Grey look a bit overdone. When other members hinted at this Grey flatly announced that Mrs. Spalding must have had some help with her fish. That wiped out his club membership.

I certainly don't want to go into the politics of angling clubs, but in this case it indicates the rebellious nature of Grey's fishing. And it has been the rebels of history that move into new fields—or waters, in this case.

In the Catalina days Grey did much of his fishing from a 38-footer, skippered by Captain Dan Danielson. It carried both engine and sail. After that he owned several rather pretentious fishing boats that took him anywhere in the world he thought the fishing would be good. By the 1930s he was equipped with a sail and motor yacht that had been built for Kaiser Wilhelm II, but its maintenance was a little steep, even for Zane Grey.

As soon as sportfishing boats went offshore, new tactics and equipment emerged. "Baiting" swordfish involves showing them a bait while they are finning on the surface. To sight such fish and manipulate the bait, the fisherman or boat captain needs a high perch. Grey's device was a crow's nest on a mast, ancestor of the tuna tower which came into use in the 1950s. The flying bridge, an elevated control center, was in use in the 30s, and the true tuna tower carried a third set of controls. Grey would hook his fish from the tower and then descend to some sort of fighting chair in the cockpit.

Early photos of Grey show him using a shoulder harness, probably leather, with a chain to support the rod. With the rod butt anchored firmly, the fish's pull could be transferred to the fisherman's upper back and shoulders. The modern fighting chair design is credited to Harlan Major in the 1930s.

Captain George Farnsworth introduced kite fishing to the modern

Fishing piers have gone to sea on many American coasts.
When fishing is good, rules against standing on railings
are likely to be ignored.

offshore scene, using kites on California tuna about 1909. He'd experimented with them somewhat earlier. South Sea Islanders (who were early users of the spoon, too) had been flying kites for a long time to carry bait where they didn't want to go with their canoes. Farnsworth wanted his bait farther away from the boat's exhaust and wake.

The kite had a special attraction other than simply getting the attractor a long way from a boat. It could skip the bait—a maneuver which proved attractive first to tuna and then to other species. There have been two basic systems, one with the kite attached to the fishing line so that it separates in case of a strike. The other involves separate lines, with the fishing line dropping clear at the strike.

Getting to the beginning of outriggers is almost impossible because they are simply specialized booms. Heavy outrigger poles were used for freshwater trolling more than 100 years ago. Tommy Gifford, one of the best and best known of the offshore skippers of the period immediately before and after World War II, is sometimes credited with developing the modern flexible outrigger (first in cane and later in metal), but numerous jury rigs were in use before that. He built 45-footers of duraluminum in 1934.

The flexible outrigger served the same purpose as the kite, skipping the bait as the trolling boat rolled in the seas. In some cases it handled baits too heavy to be worked efficiently from a rod. At first most outriggers carried teasers and baited hooks followed, trolled from the stern. Then came a clothespin arrangement with the fishing line itself suspended from the waving boom. Sleds were used around the turn of the century to carry lines over water a trolling boat couldn't cross.

Zane Grey probably invented the teaser as an offshore attractor, although nitpickers may say it is nothing more than an adaptation of the decoy used by aborigines who waited at ice holes with spears. At first the saltwater teasers were baitfish. Later, "teaser" usually meant a hookless artificial capable of violent maneuvers—more violent than the bait was capable of. A teaser puts fish in a striking mood, and lures fish into range of ultra-light tackle when a lure is too small to attract attention on its own or cannot be cast far enough.

Although the "party boat," or "head boat," was not fully developed until we had advanced electronics, the idea is quite old. Nineteenth-century skippers made excursions to bottom fishing areas, carrying

Boat rods lashed to the rail of a party boat to establish positions for their users when the boat stops.

large parties of paying customers. These fishermen used a wide variety of rods and reels as well as handlines. Most of those vessels were not specifically equipped for the job, being in the nature of "excursion ships." Much later, party boats were built around the most sophisticated electronic gear.

Such equipment is even more important on bottom boats than on trolling cruisers, for the latter will eventually pass over or through good areas by chance. A skipper on an anchored bottom boat must know exactly where he is in order to produce consistently. He looks for dropoffs, submerged wrecks, "rockpiles" and actual schools of fish. His file of such things is enormous, even though much of it may be in his head.

The "fishing barge," intended for inshore use and less mobile than the deep-water bottom boats, was an institution before 1940, making its biggest appeal on the West Coast. Anchored for long periods at one location, it could acquire its own group of local fishes. It was not confined to salt water. A crappie barge with bait troughs, blazing electric lights and the conveniences of home appeared on freshwater impoundments. Such barges, complete with lunchrooms, amount to movable fishing piers on either salt water or fresh.

While multi-millionaires outfitted one-of-a-kind cruisers for blue water and a few occasional anglers rented places at the rails of party boats, some of the best of freshwater fishermen began to probe the ocean's very edge more thoroughly. This started tentatively with the New England striper clubs, and the same fish was responsible for a later tribe of surfmen. It was gradually being learned that most of the fish were near shore and in brackish estuaries anyway.

Transportation was a key to the best surf fishing, for the caster must move with the fish. "Bass boats" were present before World War II, the "bass" meaning striper. Their purpose was to move just outside the surf line, a tour that often required a bit of nerve. Some were quite fast, a few being powered with the biggest outboard engines of their time. They were used on both Pacific and Atlantic coasts. There were a few beach buggies too, elemental converisons of cars and trucks. The Model A Ford was a good subject for such "improvements."

Remember that the striped bass had been pretty well absent from the New England coast between about 1900 and the 1930s. North Atlantic fishermen welcomed it back with enthusiasm, but a World War interfered with the reception. Not until Johnny came marching home did a new breed of surf caster really come into its own. New England anglers were leaders in surf fishing and the gear that went with it. Frank Woolner and Hal Lyman, editor and publisher of *Salt Water Sportsman,* became a national voice of coastal fishermen, mainly from New England's steep beaches.

The beach buggy needed power for running on sand and it needed big flotation tires, tires that performed best when soft. Model A Fords gradually gave way to more modern vehicles, notably the step-in van. It had unique qualities for hauling the things surf fishermen need as well as the fishermen themselves. And for some reason it could (with big tires) navigate soft sand, dry or wet. For some years coastal delivery men had a waiting list of buyers for their used vans. The Model A's led the parade during the 1940s, but vans came on in the 50s and the live-aboard rig became common.

At first, onboard cooking facilities burned gasoline and then went to butane. Rod holders were some of the first essentials. A beach buggy with enormous Calcutta or Burma cane rods sticking skyward or at odd angles resembled a crab from another galaxy.

The beachcombing buggy jockeys acquired skills and techniques

Model A Ford beach buggy used by Frank and Richard Wolner in mid 1940s before the vans became popular.
(Photo by Frank Woolner)

unheard of until the boom after World War II. They read the sloughs and runouts of an ever-changing coastal world and coined their own terminology for the high surf. The frantic feeding of large numbers of striped bass sweeping into the breakers was a "blitz," a name borrowed from Hitler's cross-nation dashes.

The military Jeep found a ready place on the sands as a sort of stripped-down, ultra-mobile specialist. But it needed big tires, and it was some time before manufacturers could produce anything that would replace a big truck or aircraft tire partly deflated. In fact, to this day, the first move on a treacherous beach is to let out some air. Portable compressors were almost standard equipment and are still popular.

By the 60s, 4-wheel-drive trucks and wagons built by most of the leading car manufacturers began to move in on the improvised buggies, even though showroom models often needed some modification.

Not everything went smoothly for the surfman. His chief trouble came from the hangers-on who decided the real game was running the beach and jumping the dunes rather than fishing. As beach buggies and dune buggies appeared by the thousands, beach residents unhappily viewed rutted and blowing sand dunes. Sunbathers were forced to leap for their lives. It wasn't the fishermen, it was mechanized vandals, and the surf anglers had to do something. The Massachusetts Beach Buggy Association was the first of a number of such groups that tried to appease sedentary beach lovers, police their own ranks and make things tough for the outlaws. In the meantime, some irate feminine buggy haters dug a beach-buggy trap and camouflaged it. Crash!

Beach travel problems will probably never be completely resolved but responsible organizations have gone a long way toward it.

With advanced aluminum fabrication came a new kind of surf boat, a light outboard that could be launched through the surf and later racked atop a buggy. The technique of launching in surf requires resolute action, a judgment of the wave series and an oarsman who catches water without a fluff.

Set the boat on the beach, shove it in with the right wave, row like hell and get the motor started. If things aren't exactly right the fishing party and equipment become instant flotsam. This method was truly

*By the 1950s the surfman's beach buggy was often
living quarters as well as transportation.
The converted step-in van was revolutionary and the aluminum
surf boat extended the angler's range.
(Photo by Frank Woolner)*

gilded when some experts learned to launch bigger boats of trailer size, even 18-footers, by giving the critical shove with the prow of the beach buggy.

The surf fisherman became a proud individualist, and for good reason. Anyone who has looked up at a crashing comber by starlight can appreciate the real and imagined dangers of a lonely beach at night. Surfmen became pretty rough customers, unshaven and unbathed during good fishing times when they lived on the beach, a little weatherbeaten and red-eyed when they got back to the office.

After spinning tackle came in it was some years before it could truly compete with the turning spool and heavy baits. Although many fishermen used spinning reels for their lighter fishing, they clung to reels such as the durable Penn Squidder when the bait was heavy and the fish a long way off. Things evened up somewhat later as spinning lines improved. The early turning-spool lines had been Cuttyhunk linen, hot on the thumb, prone to throw a shower of salt water when wet and requiring constant care.

Surf fishermen, of course, began with striped bass, but caught many other species, including bluefish, seatrout and channel bass. They often used eels and eelskins, but those baits have been largely replaced by plastic. They threw squids and jigs and some outsize plugs that were offshoots of freshwater bass baits.

The bay and back-country fishermen had operated quietly for many years using black bass tackle. The high-quality baitcasting reel and steel or bamboo rod had done well on striped bass, weakfish, channel bass (redfish) and even tarpon for some time before World War II. The only concession to abrasive saltwater fish had been wire leaders. Saltwater fly fishing moved pretty slowly because the better fly rods were bamboo and were extremely heavy when capable of handling what would now be called a No. 10 or 11 line. Such numbers weren't used in those days, and a heavy line would be something like a GAAAF.

The nearest to a manufactured tool for heavy duty saltwater fly fishing was a two-handed salmon rod, and it wasn't well adapted to the rough-and-tumble demands of ocean use.

The outboard motor had a long way to go before it was truly reliable for the back-country of San Francisco Bay or the Florida Keys (such fishing had hardly been touched). When it came on strongly after the war it was encouraged by "discovery" of some fish that had been known for a long time but had never received much attention. Most of them were southerners. Tarpon seemed made for the new light tackle, which included spinning gear. Snook were supercharged targets for shoreline bass fishermen and bonefish were reintroduced as spinning and flyfishing trophies.

The bonefish was a sort of scaled rumor for almost a century. It had been freely confused with the ladyfish, which it resembles in appearance. Dr. James Henshall, usually a reliable source on fishes and fishing, confused the two, even after he spoke of first-hand experience. In one of his works a bonefish is pictured as a ladyfish and a ladyfish is misnamed a bonefish. But the mixup didn't end there, for Henshall describes the great leaping qualities of both species. The ladyfish, which doesn't gain nearly the size of the bonefish, *is* a wild leaper, making short runs. The bonefish that leaps would be an oddity and would probably require a ramp, for the bone simply doesn't operate that way. He just hurries.

Exploratory fishermen such as Zane Grey and his brother had built a strong base for bonefish fables when they attempted to catch them

Once they learned it better, fishermen went to lighter tackle for tarpon. This one is hooked on a glass fly rod.

141

on rather heavy tackle and reported breaking almost everything but the oars. From what I read into Grey's published report, he apparently attempted to stop the bonefish without letting them run (it's likely that their gear didn't adapt well to high-speed takeoffs on a shallow flat). I suspect the first true bonefish experts passed on without ever telling their story, because few sportsmen of 1918 were interested in stalking a bone-filled fish in 9 inches of water.

The limited bonefish craze that struck in the late 40s and early 50s did a great deal for light tackle saltwater fishing, even though there never were many bonefishermen. Once an angler hooked a bonefish he was inclined to doubt the old motto of Henshall, that the black bass was "ounce for ounce and pound for pound the gamest fish that swims."

There are claims of bonefish taken on a fly as far back as the 20s. Certainly there were some before 1947 when the boom started. Two Floridians, Joe Brooks and Allen Corson, gave the bonefish its start as a real fly rod target. Corson was fishing editor of the *Miami Herald* and Brooks was executive secretary of the Miami Metropolitan Fishing Tournament. For a time the bonefish and its foibles were a passion of Brooks, who was already nationally known as a fly fisherman and outdoor writer. Brooks, ex-boxer, top-notch golfer, long-time fly caster and angling traditionalist, filled outdoor publications with bonefish stories and moved to the Florida Keys to be near his catch. Ted Williams of baseball fame didn't hurt their image either. Williams, who had taken an interest in fly casting, was expertly throwing flies at sportsmen's shows and attracted members of the general sporting press. By the time they got through praising the bonefish it had become a sizzling wraith capable of 70 miles an hour on the flats and generally caught by casts of more than 100 feet.

The bonefish can't swim 70 miles an hour and is often caught by 40-foot casts, and it didn't need all of that hyperbole to be a spectacular addition to the fly fisherman's repertoire. Bonefishing came when spinning was just getting a good start. It's an ideal subject for spinning gear and small jigs. For every fly fisherman who caught a bonefish there were dozens of spinfishermen.

Tarpon were easily accessible by almost any kind of skiff, and the postwar outboards added new speed and reliability. At first the big thing was "baby" tarpon, those under 20 pounds or so (some said anything under 50 was a baby). Then the shallow water fishermen saw the possibilities of catching tarpon of 100 pounds or more on fly tackle. Joe Brooks was prominent in this, at one time holding a world record well over the 100 mark. He was guided that time by Stuart Apte, who later became a leading contender both as guide and angler.

Saltwater fishing has long involved big-fish records, regulated by the International Game Fish Association since 1940. But this big-league fly fishing was a new game. No worldwide specifications had been set for fly tackle, that business being left up to individual tournaments. Then the Saltwater Flyrodders Association was formed in 1965.

At first, Brooks the traditionalist said that the use of a heavy shock tippet was not fly fishing. He practiced what he preached and for years he had played all saltwater fish on an ordinary leader tippet. Of course he lost most of his really big fish through leader abrasion. When he caught his big tarpon with Apte, he had gone to a shock tippet.

Another famous fly fisherman, Lee Wulff, became known for de-

*Light plugcasting gear went to salt water with the
"Cub" accessory drag handle, shown here with Pflueger Supreme reel
and bluefish.*

clining some of the modern developments. He caught big fish on what he called "standard" fly tackle—without the modern heavy-duty rods and reels.

The accepted shock tippet on the fly rod was a breakthrough because it opened up a new world to people casting big feathers and heavy lines. Some tippets were made of leader wire, but heavy monofilament was almost universally accepted later on. The exceptions were with really toothy specimens such as barracuda.

Until the big tarpon days, most fly reels, even the outsized winches used by Atlantic salmon fishermen, had been incapable of standing long runs by heavy fish. Some of the giant brass salmon reels of the 19th century had great line capacity but lacked drag refinements and were intended for two-handed operation with giant rods. A good example was the Malloch. Although the name crops up more commonly in connection with the beginnings of spinning, it meant quality tackle long before that.

At about the time it became routine to take a 100-pound tarpon on a fly, bar stock aluminum saltwater reels such as the Fin Nor and the Seamaster, both produced near the action in Miami, were introduced. With these reels the fly fisherman had a pretty good shot at anything he could get to strike. Teasing techniques improved for the next 30 years. Combine teasers, thick-walled glass rods, heavy duty reels and judiciously applied chum lines, and hardly anything that swims is safe from an ambitious feather merchant.

This is beginning to sound as if heavy-duty fly fishing is only a Florida product. Many of the necessary fish did live there, but the actual *casting* of long, heavy lines advanced more on the West Coast where the 100-foot cast was needed for steelhead and Pacific salmon. Not only did the West Coasters win most casting tournaments, they worked out methods for getting a fly down deep, an area fly fishermen had never bothered with before. It was the combination of California casting and Florida fishing that put the big fly rod "on the map."

Three environmental problems closed in on coastal fishermen in 1960. Pollution, which had been a largely unnoticed problem since the first factories were built, ended river runs of some anadromous fish. The extent of its effect farther offshore remained unknown, but was recognized in both commercial and sport fishing. Clean-up of coastal

*Modern surf equipment is used by Frank Woolner (left)
and Curt Gowdy. Woolner, "sachem of the high surf," has
been through the transition from Calcutta poles to glass.*

waters began with the environmental enthusiasm of the 60s. Improvement was noticed almost immediately, but while things got better in some areas, they worsened in others.

Two other problems were even tougher. One was the development of coastal marshes, which greatly reduced the productivity of the brackish zone, now recognized as the most fertile of all. By the 70s some coastal regulations had teeth, but much damage was already done. The dredging and filling of what had once been considered worthless swamps was hard to stop, especially in view of the high value placed on seaside properties.

The third difficulty, an irreversible trend, is simply an increased need for fresh water, a need which has changed subterranean water supplies, allowed salt water intrusion far inland and reduced the extent of the invaluable brackish zone. Outstanding examples have been the thirst of fast-growing California, which has in some cases actually siphoned off the incubation waters of the striped bass in San Francisco Bay, and the settlement of the Florida Everglades, which has robbed the mangrove coasts of the southern peninsula's freshwater runoff.

Assessment of saltwater fishery resources is almost impossible. One reason is the increased efficiency of fishermen. Better boats and tackle, and especially the use of sophisticated electronic equipment, make it possible to catch a larger percentage of the existing fish. Comparisons with catches of a few years ago are hardly a true indication of total supply.

As saltwater fishing entered the 1980s, more fishermen than ever before were out with more boats and more know-how. Except for the billfishes, not many saltwater catches were being turned back, but it seemed likely that the catch-and-release policy growing inland would some day also be essential offshore.

CHAPTER NINE

SOME BIOLOGY

Wherever fishermen go they tend to take their favorite fish with them. This barrel and bucket philosophy has resulted in some of the world's finest fishing and some of the worst ecological disasters.

Not all fishermen agree as to an ideal gamefish and not all understand the delicate balances that make high-quality sport. Fisheries biology was primitive or non-existent when many of the big manmade changes took place. Today, even in a relatively advanced scientific climate, room still exists for violent disagreement, for clandestine fish plantings and complete retreats from earlier policies.

In some cases, as with wild trout and salmon streams and estuarine brackish water, fishing territory has shrunk appallingly. In another field, that of impounded waters, there is more habitat and more resident fish than ever before. The chattering trout and smallmouth streams that were obliterated by the big dams have been supplanted by deep acres that support more fish than the streams ever did—whether the actual fishing quality is better or not. There's disagreement about that.

Colonial settlement was serious business—too serious to be concerned with Atlantic salmon or Long Island trout. The ecological effect was destructive, as is often the case with pioneer invasions. A family fighting for survival wouldn't have listened anyway, even if the effect indiscriminate development would have on natural resources had been known.

Put bluntly, the colonists raped the countryside. They destroyed the timber, wore out the soil and polluted the rivers. But let's not be pious. We'd probably do the same thing over again; it is being done on frontiers of every continent of the world. Few of us are so high-minded as to trade our personal welfare for the sport of a later generation.

Deterioration of Eastern fish populations accelerated with the first sawmill, the first factory and the first steamboat. The loss of the Atlantic salmon was noted first because it was a large fish and because it had been a staple of diet. We read also, as mentioned earlier, that salmon were used for fertilizer and also fed to cattle. Hogs would thrive on fish. Of course small trout streams were obliterated or silted

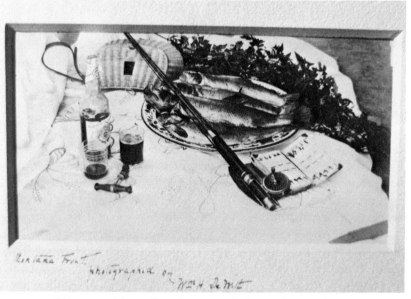

"Montana Trout," a photograph from about 1890.
(Photo courtesy of The Museum of American Fly Fishing, Inc.)

in by eroding hillsides, but that wasn't dramatic enough to be reported. Most colonists considered sport fishing frivolous. They might
have been Indian killers and witch burners but, by golly, they didn't
fritter away their time.

By about the middle of the 19th century Atlantic salmon had virtually disappeared from their haunts in the industrial East, and were
gone from the southern coasts. They were still found in the Maine
rivers and in Canadian rivers farther north.

Sewage and factory refuse supplemented by the discharges of commercial shipping polluted waters near population centers, and the
lumber industry was almost as destructive in less crowded surroundings. Cutover slopes eroded and log drives on large rivers had their
own effect. Through the years an accumulation of sunken bark
turned to bottom sludge that wouldn't support gamefish.

When water quality deteriorated because of silting, shallowing and
an attendant warming, some fish faded rapidly. In Maine, for example, native brook trout were unable to cope with water conditions in many of the bigger streams. Rainbow and brown trout
were tried as substitutes and tolerant smallmouth and largemouth
bass were introduced, "warm-water fishes" whereas trout are "cold-
water fish."

Although the new fish filled the gap to some extent, many die-hard
brook trout fishermen refused to accept them. The bass, especially,
drew the ire of former trout fishermen, a displeasure that has carried
over 100 years. Even today, some Maine residents scorn bass as
"tourist fish."

"Oh, bass are all right, I guess," a resort owner told me in 1970.
"There's a man in Portland who eats the damned things!"

A rustic who didn't realize the bass is America's favorite fish? Of
course not. He just wouldn't admit it.

Michigan's history was similar to Maine's when lumbering and
other industry degraded cold, clean streams. The Michigan grayling is
gone forever. It had to have very pure, cold water. The brook trout
took over where the grayling could not survive, and rainbow and
brown trout supplanted the brookie in much of its range.

So plantings have often been misguided efforts, but without them
we would have more barren waters. A running chronology is unsatis-
factory in a history of fishes, for some principal characters came in

late. The brown trout, now a resident of much of the world, is such a character and has had a great influence on American angling.

The brown grows large in both lake and stream, is capable of withstanding warmer and more polluted water than the brook trout or the grayling, and is highly regarded by fly fishermen for its surface feeding in the larger sizes when conditions are right. It is considered the most intelligent of trouts. Often big browns can be found in streams considered "dead" as far as salmonids are concerned. Given a proper season or two the browns will reestablish.

It was the brown trout that for hundreds of years challenged European fishermen. As an imported salmonid it has been a rousing success, despite the wails of those who love only "natives," whichever species they might be.

Fish beauty is in the eye of the beholder. At various times I have heard rainbow, brown, brook and cutthroat each called the most beautiful fish of all. But anyone having a grudge against a fish is likely to say nasty things. I love the description of a brown trout as stated by Benjamin Kent in 1902. Addicted to the Eastern brook trout, Kent wrote, "In appearance the brown is scaly, flat, greenish yellow, irregular in form, bad eye, homely all over."

The brown trout had done a great deal of migrating before it reached the United States. After some failures due to lack of refrigeration of the eggs on the long voyage, it was finally established in Tasmania in 1864, and later on the Australian mainland and New Zealand. By 1892 the fish had been established in Africa. Browns came to the U.S. in 1883 after Fred Mather, fish culturist and writer, made arrangements with Baron Lucius von Behr of Germany.

German browns were planted in Argentina in 1904 and in Chile in 1905—fisheries "discovered" much later by Americans.

Careful tests have shown the brown is harder to catch than the brookie or the rainbow, or the cutthroat of the West. In the 19th century the brown was noted as a traveler. But the American rainbow, originally found only in the far West, has gone almost everywhere the brown has.

Though the brown trout introduction was a triumph, the carp invasion was almost criminal. When the United States Fish Commission imported the carp in 1876 it came with glowing recommendations. This, said some political office holders, was a triumph for the American sportsman, and congressmen busily made arrangements to ship carp to their lucky constituents.

The carp took to our warm waters, multiplied astonishingly, stirred up the mud, destroyed vegetation and crowded desirable fish.

They soon degenerated from a prize political catch to a trash fish. We have trapped them, shot them with bows, speared them and poisoned them, but this battle is lost. Not that catching carp on hook and line with carefully prepared "doughballs" isn't clever. It just isn't what most American anglers had been waiting for.

The carp is valued in Asia, especially the Orient. It hasn't worked here. Maybe, if our more desirable fish disappear, it will fill a gap. We hope that won't be necessary.

Some other introductions may be noted with names, dates and places. The black bass spread its range in thousands of buckets and barrels and in so many directions that the explosion was almost totally unrecorded. The most important factors were railroads and the tough nature of the bass themselves, especially the largemouths.

Bass are extremely tolerant of temperature, multiply like gnats, and

Garfish, believed to consume food needed by game species,
were gigged at night by sport fishermen in the 1950s,
often as a club project.

can survive for considerable periods out of water. As the railroads pushed westward in the mid-1800s, passengers and crews alike took delight in showering bass fry down from new trestles into creeks. Trains went fast enough that fish could be kept alive for considerable distances.

And the tank pond was a natural depot for black bass looking for a home. Everywhere the chuffing steam trains went there must be water for the boilers. Dam a wet-weather creek, using part of the dam as a railroad grade, and set a big tank on stilts to furnish a gravity feed. The tank pond was new habitat with the special qualities of new impoundments. What fisherman could resist sloshing some fry into such a place?

At any rate, black bass soon spread to all of the contiguous states and became America's own unique game fish. Its popularity went by spurts until the 1960s when it, and the glamorous equipment that went with it, boomed into a sportsman's obsession. By then many times more bass were alive and well than Columbus could have found if he had cared. The black bass had been waiting for people.

All of America's trouts and chars have strains that go to sea. The relationship between landlocked fish and "seatrout," "salters" or steelhead has been a biological puzzle. I use the word "landlocked" loosely, because many of the trouts that stay inland are really "locked" by untenable water. For example, a thousand creeks and rivers that feed the Mississippi have trout populations connected to the oceans by broad waterways. But in order to reach the sea they would have to use water that is too warm or of quality too low for trout welfare.

The rainbow, originally a resident of the western watersheds, is evidently a seagoing fish like the Atlantic salmon, but its landlocked population is much greater than that of the salmon. Anyway, it appears the steelhead evolved inland rather than the other way around. It is a very close relative of the Atlantic salmon, more closely related to it than to the Pacific salmons, which spawn only once. Some Asiatic trout are closely related to American rainbows.

The rainbow is the most valued of our native trout for easily stated reasons. Most important, it has adapted beautifully to new waters, and thus has found its way to virtually all cool streams and lakes of the continent. In its way, it is as tough a customer as the brown trout

Some Biology

with high tolerance for warmth and pollution—and it is the darling of hatcheries. They say you can "raise rainbows like chickens." That may be an exaggeration, but the rainbow is a good bet and can sometimes survive in water above 80 degrees.

Since rainbows grow to widely different sizes dependent upon habitat, and take on all sorts of unusual colors, it is easy to give them a variety of names. The steelhead was long considered a different fish from the stay-at-home rainbow. Arguments went on for generations, spiced by the extra strength and speed generated by silvery fresh-run migrants. Finally, fish culturists learned that the steelhead was simply a rainbow trout with a seagoing makeup. All rainbows tend to work upstream to spawn.

Some watersheds produce much larger steelheads than others, even though they all enter the sea at about the same time and place. For example, the Babine and Kispiox rivers of British Columbia, tributaries of the Skeena, have long been noted for giant steelhead caught on the fly. Other Skeena tributaries, some of them larger waterways than either of the two prize-winning rivers, have steelhead that average much smaller. The Kamloops trout, a really successful landlock rainbow, grows to great size in northwestern lakes.

Trout cross-breed, and a special strain can vanish in a few generations. The brilliant-hued golden trout, for example, was originally found only in the high Kern River area of California. Generally accepted as a special rainbow isolated by rugged terrain, it has been successfully transplanted in dozens of waters in mountain country. But release the golden with "ordinary" lowland rainbows and the gaudy colors will disappear.

Sport fishermen are inclined to yawn at the nitpicking studies of taxonomists. It certainly didn't make much difference at first, for in the last century and the first part of this one it was enough to get a rainbow trout, or any other species, from native waters to a new home. Now, with modern facilities for hatching and transporting, the possibilities are almost endless. If Babine river steelhead are bigger than those in the Bulkley river, why not increase the fish size in some California creek? Such thoughts are no longer far-fetched.

Today, no one in the United States is very far from trout fishing. For example, brook trout, originally located from the Mississippi eastward and south to Georgia's mountains, have moved up and west-

153

ward to the high lakes and streams. Much of their original home has gone the way of silt and sewage, but their overall range is greatly enlarged. Find pure cold water today, and chances are the brookie will be there. Seth Green, revered pioneer of scientific fish culture, established a brook trout hatchery in New York in 1864. Brookies have spread out on an international scale ever since.

The brook trout, like the other chars, is distinguished from true trout by somewhat different scales, and especially by fewer teeth on the vomerine bone on the roof of the mouth. The arctic char is certainly a good gamefish, but is unknown to most anglers because of its Far North residence. The lake trout, gray trout, Mackinaw or togue remains important over most of Canada and has an interesting history in the Great Lakes. It hasn't been introduced successfully to any cool creek, but has been crossed with the brook trout to produce the *splake.*

The cutthroat trouts of the West, unique because of their many sub-species, a result of natural mountain barriers, have not been widely distributed and tend to lose their identity when placed in rain-

The striped bass, adapting to fresh water as well as salt, became a prize of 20th century fish management. These are from New Jersey.

bow waters. The hybrid that results may have a rainbow's predominant coloration with the addition of faint red slashes at the throat. Cutthroat are sporting fish but seldom jump when hooked, lacking some of the fire of the native rainbow or the brown.

While black bass fry traveled in coffee pots and milk cans, and fishery drivers raced through the mountains with primitive equipment and gasping trout, a pair of eastern species took some long trips.

The American shad, an anadromous fish of the eastern seaboard from New England to Florida, was an early target of fly fishermen, but was democratic enough that during some of their Potomac runs hungry local people could catch them with a rag on a hook. In 1871, the shad made a big jump to the Pacific Coast, where it was a happy subject for fly casters 100 years later, even though they sometimes called them "stink salmon." Seth Green, who appears so regularly in most early accounts of fish culture, handled the shad planting.

The striped bass went west too. As a coastal resident this "fisherman's fish" has a record of long-term population fluctuations. Whole generations of striped bass fishermen have been followed by periods in which their descendents never saw a "rockfish." For 30 years after the striper clubs left the New England coast, the striper was almost unknown in its old haunts. Then it came back. The result was a new breed of surf fishermen, proud, unshaven, red-eyed beach buggy jockeys with rods that would have intimidated the stand anglers of 1870.

Keep an eye on this striped bass business. It's been big fishing news and it's going to stay big news.

To begin with, the striper, individually, is pretty delicate. Fisheries workers have found striped bass belly-up after handling that a largemouth bass would hardly notice. Also, the striped bass is anadromous. It spawns in freshwater rivers and then goes to sea. The eggs drift freely in moving water until hatching. Such a life history is full of hazards.

The striper was moved to the Pacific Coast in 1886 and has held forth at times from the Columbia River to Los Angeles. I say "at times" because populations of the western fish have been almost as erratic as its eastern ancestors.

Best known of the Pacific striper areas has been the San Francisco

Bay region, where they are caught in water that varies from "completely fresh" to "completely salt." Those are handy terms, although quite inaccurate. Pacific anglers are strong on fly fishing with heavy rods and long lines. Fly fishing for stripers has been down their alley, so the sport is well documented and boosted by prize fish taken on bugs and streamers.

The North Pacific fish have gone up and down in typical striper fashion without explanation. San Francisco Bay fish have fallen upon hard times for more obvious reasons. Russell Chatham, Pacific Coast angling pundit, explains that the San Francisco Bay water has been drawn off to serve California's bulging population.

"The ditches to Los Angeles are full of little striped bass," Chatham says. As touchy as they are to handle, striped bass are a prize of fishery management. A successful striped bass hatchery was in operation on the Roanoke River of North Carolina before 1900.

Santee-Cooper Reservoir in South Carolina was big news in striped bass fishing. About 1948 it was discovered that the stripers imprisoned by hydro-electric damming of the river were spawning successfully in fresh water without ever going to sea. However accidental, this was a major breakthrough.

About 20 years later, advanced management showed that stripers could be tailored to special purposes by being crossed with the white bass, a much smaller freshwater fish of more limited sport value. The new fish could withstand very warm fresh water, grew much larger than the white bass and could be taken by sporting methods. By the late 70s striped bass of one kind or another were thriving in fresh waters across the country, spreading almost as the black bass had once done, but with a more scientific approach. In fact, the fish had outdistanced fishing methods, and serious inland anglers had gone back to the drawing board to equip themselves for the new challenge.

Fish plantings of recent years have been aimed at overfished areas or degraded waters where native fish have disappeared or been reduced in numbers. This is especially important in coastal areas. It was a long time before the importance of brackish water marshes was understood. Their drainage and development have been a sneak punch at sport as well as commercial fisheries.

Apart from the anadromous fish which have so complex a life pattern that biologists cannot even trace it, some species live habitually

*Silver salmon or coho, caught on light spinning gear
in an Alaska creek.*

in *either* fresh or salt water for long periods and seem to have ill-defined migration programs. These are of special interest to researchers, for although no one is hoping to establish swordfish in South Dakota, any fish that can adapt to either fresh or salt water is likely to fill a gap.

Cautious biologists can also see advantages in fish that do not reproduce. Artificially spawned populations can be allowed to die out if unwanted at a later date. The snook, a tropical and sub-tropical fish found mainly in Florida within the United States, can live in fresh water although it is believed to spawn only in salt. Since 1974, artificial snook spawning has proved practical; it should be a good gamefish for very warm inland waters. Like many other such projects, artificially spawned snook await only the funds for appropriate hatcheries, assuming that satisfactory homes for the fish can be found.

Strong populations of artificially spawned fish are the mainstay of some famous fisheries. In the cold tailwaters of numerous hydro-electric dams, large trout that can't reproduce there have been a welcome substitute for the black bass that were "frozen out" by cold discharges. A large share of the populations in "wild" trout lakes do not reproduce. Most famous of all are the Pacific salmon that saved Great Lakes sport fishing.

Like many other stories of fish and nature, the Great Lakes tale is an incredibly long one, covering some 175 years. It began when the Welland Canal opened in 1829, bypassing Niagara Falls and leaving a direct water route from the lakes to the Atlantic. It took more than 100 years, but lamprey eels worked their way to the lakes and attacked the lake trout, the leading game and commercial fish of the region. In the 30s fishing remained good but mischief was afoot.

The eels are parasites with suction mouths, feeding on flesh and blood of their hosts. Aided by uncontrolled pollution (the extent and effects of the pollution are indistinct and sometimes argued), the eels ruined the lake trout fishery. With the lake trout almost gone, the alewife, a small resident "baitfish," proliferated. It soon died by the millions, and the beaches smelled worse than any pollution had caused them to.

Weirs and both mechanical and electrical traps were tried, but the lampreys were finally stopped by selective poisoning. By the 60s it appeared the eels were under control, and in the meantime residents of the lake shores had been cleaning up their act. The lakes were ready to start over.

Pacific salmon were tried, a project that had failed earlier. In 1964, Dr. Howard Tanner and Dr. Wayne Tody secured silver salmon (coho) eggs from Oregon and released smolts in Michigan streams in 1966. Fishing exploded into the biggest angling news of the 60s. The salmon could not reproduce on their own but they feasted on the millions of alewives, fattened quickly and smashed trolling spoons with enthusiasm.

At first there was a complication in "imprinting" fish to return to a chosen location at spawning time. It was necessary to keep them for some time in waters they were expected to return to, or they'd be "lost." Eventually, a system of imprinting was developed in the hatchery, and the salmon would make their spawning runs to almost any creek desired, a triumph of nature manipulation.

The salmon business was on a rampage. Tackle companies listed pages of medium-heavy gear designated as coho this or that. Tourist business on the lake shores boomed and new chartermen went into action. But there were some hitches.

The presence of big fish in plenty brought what Patrick K. Snook calls an "insanity period." Calm days are deceptive on the big lakes, and despite urgent warnings by the Coast Guard many skippers of the mill-pond fleet tried to ride out a squall in the fall of 1967. Seven fishermen drowned, hospitals were crowded and hundreds of boats were demolished. After that, fishing expeditions were less amateurish.

After the cohos came the king or chinook salmon, and it now seems that the Great Lakes are quite capable of handling almost any of the Pacific salmons—with stocking.

An ethical question also arose. Snagging salmon during their upstream spawning runs is denounced by many, but the fish will die anyway and under certain circumstances cannot be caught by more sporting means. The subject continues to draw argument.

There are a great many gamefish in the Great Lakes besides the Pacific salmon, but the big news is the salmon triumph. We're just getting started in a business that seems limitless.

Fish management is more than hatching fish. Dealing with fishing pressures, often intensified by reduced fishing area, becomes a con-

tinuing question of regulation and law enforcement spliced with habitat preservation, improvement and acquisition. Serious fish culture
began in America more than 100 years ago, but it was primitive.
Regulations and law enforcement began long before that.

Through the years we have suffered from fads, some of them accepted by dedicated scientists. Take the hatchery syndrome.

The hatchery is a mainstay of fish management, but it is not the
cure-all. Seth Green is said to have raised 20 species of fish. In the last
century it looked as if they had the answer.

Moving fish from one area to another was the backbone of our
trout fishing. Without hatcheries and fish introductions we might be
out of business now, but a few times we got carried away. Put-and-
take fishing is what keeps many waters going. Pallid hatchery rainbows looking for marshmallows and canned corn are much better
than no fish at all.

When top-notch hatchery strains were developed it was obvious
that a given stream or lake could have all the fish we could afford to
plant—temporarily. Hatchery fish don't necessarily do well in the

Northern pike, scorned by some as an aquatic roughneck,
remain a reliable target for a variety of methods from
trolling to fly casting.

wild. In many cases they tend to disappear if not caught quickly, and in order to provide easy catches for casual fishermen we need a quantity beyond what the habitat can support.

A hundred years ago the purpose of the hatchery was to produce fingerlings. Later it was found that a more practical way was to raise keeper-size fish, and the hatchery truck comedy was the eventual result. Fishermen would get a tip as to where a batch of trout was to be dumped, and the tank truck would lead a parade. Freshly dumped into strange waters, the dazed and stupid trout would be pounced upon almost instantly by eager fishermen. Without the hatchery trout, some of the areas would have no fish at all. It is artificial, but it is fishing of sorts. And it costs a great deal of money.

Trouble also existed with adding hatchery trout to waters that already contained wild fish. (By "wild" fish I mean those that are reproducing, even though they may have originated in hatchery stock.) Many serious trout fishermen didn't want to catch "tame" fish. They wanted money spent for improving habitat rather than the hatchery product. On the other side of the table was (and still is) a part of the tourist industry that needs easily caught hatchery fish to attract once-a-year vacation anglers.

Economy seemed to be on the side of the serious anglers, but in the 1970s a new spectre appeared on the hatchery horizon. Biologists reported that not only did hatchery fish disappear if they weren't soon caught, but that wild fish populations were greatly reduced when the new fish were released. Apparently it was a kind of overcrowding, and even though wild fish might be tougher and more energetic, they retreated from the invasion.

Hatcheries now have better defined roles. They are needed to replace a fishery that has been ruined by natural causes or over-fishing, and are essential in producing put-and-take fisheries (expensive). They also provide services for anadromous fishes whose natural spawning runs have been blocked by dams or development, as along the Pacific Coast. They maintain fisheries such as the salmon of the Great Lakes and trout fishing below big dams. They are strongly opposed as constant supplements to wild fish, and here is a changing concept.

For many years biologists insisted that hook-and-line fishing could not harm black bass waters. Black bass hatcheries fell into disfavor for it was rightly stated that one female bass could repopulate a lake or river if her progeny lived.

But when fishing became poor in spite of pure water, where had the bass gone? In the 1970s it was finally confessed that in some lakes the fishermen were catching too many. Tagging proved that too many of certain sizes were caught, leaving a lake with a few hard-to-find monsters, a great many tiny fish, and a decreasing number of the in-between sizes that make up a desirable harvest. Now, after long preaching that bass size limits were unnecessary, biologists recommended them. Tentative moves toward "slot limits" that permitted harvest of larger and smaller fish were implemented, and this seems to be working.

Impoundments have always had a boom-and-bust history, exceptional fishing when the lake is new, then a period of very slow fishing, and possibly a recovery later on.

One new aid to black bass welfare is the draw-down, a system adopted for lakes that have become too fertile as a result of sewage or agricultural runoff. At one time it was believed a constant water level was best, but dramatic things have been achieved temporarily by lowering a lake's level, exposing its shores to sunlight for a period, and then allowing it to refill.

One exotic fish was getting a hard look in 1980. The amur or grass carp, a European and Asiatic import, was being considered as a weedeater for southern waters. Too much vegetation had come from a rich nutrient supply.

Since the grass carp grows quite large and is believed capable of displacing gamefish species there have been legal battles. It's now possible to hatch grass carp that cannot reproduce, so if no damage has already been done the fish managers can breathe a sigh of relief.

Most of the dangerous exotics have come in from the South. The walking catfish was a feared invader of a few years back, but as with many other undesirables, its northward travel has been halted by cold weather. Most of the other menaces, such as piranha, have been confined to a rather apprehensive south Florida, the main gateway from Latin America. Cold seems to be a better barrier than U.S. Customs.

CHAPTER TEN

WHATEVER FLOATS

Fishing boats have adapted to their varied tasks down through the centuries, but more than any other part of the angler's equipment they have developed in slightly different directions in various parts of the world.

This is confusing to the historian who finds that on a certain type of river in British Columbia anglers are using a boat that may look a great deal different from what is used in Argentina on what appears to be the same type of water. The first thought is that one or the other is more advanced, but that isn't necessarily so and the owner of each is likely to stand up for its efficiency. And newer is not necessarily better, although some types such as the bass boat and the outboard "fishing machine" have come on in the past 20 years and, in their specific niches, outdone anything that went before.

Go to the other extreme. The Indian's birchbark canoe is hard to beat for some uses. The banks dory of another century is unchallenged for small size in high seas, and with slight modification, it has found a home on the whitewater rivers. New, stronger and lighter materials have not altered the dory's silhouette.

It appears, however, that Americans have led almost all the way in fishing boat development—ever since a day at Gloucester, Massachusetts, in 1713 when a new ship came off the ways. She slid sleekly into the sea and someone shouted, "Oh, how she scoons!" *Scoon* had some British connotation of a skipping stone, and the new ship was called a *schooner.* America's sailing ships, fleet before the winds of the Seven Seas, made Americans famous as some of the world's greatest sailors and fishermen. Other smaller sailing vessels also caught fish and carried them to market. Many adopted features of the big ocean speedsters.

The dory, high at bow and stern, easy under sail or oars but treacherous when overloaded with too many cod, was the pattern for river drift boats of another era. Such a boat originally evolved from the necessity of daily launching and nesting on deck when not in use. No other design was quite so seaworthy and so light and manageable.

In 1935 two famous fishermen, Michael Lerner
(in fighting chair) and Tommy Gifford (center), landed this
broadbill off Nova Scotia, using a modified dory.
(Photo from the Michael Lerner Collection, property of the IGFA)

Saltwater sport fishermen didn't go for the dory much after the sailing days, although it stayed with commercial fishermen. There were numerous dory designs that would work with outboard motors but they were relatively slow, and speed was in demand, necessary or not. Some big game fishermen have bolted fishing chairs to dories and caught giants.

The Indian canoe, only slightly modified, is still a favorite for transportation in the north country where trout, steelhead and salmon fishermen use it for both efficiency and tradition. The Indian birchbarks and dugouts ranged from great war canoes with rows of paddleswinging braves to little one-man cockleshells that could be carried on one shoulder for a portage, making "highways" of creeks that later generations would never consider navigable. The canoe was transportation by day and shelter at night.

Big freight canoes made by French voyageurs were a final development in size. They were paddled by an unusual product of the frontier, a hardbitten race that came even before the mountain men of the early 19th century. Those French were absorbed by the wild land, and probably reached the Rockies long before Lewis and Clark. They interbred with the Indians and have kept their reputation as hunters, trappers, portagers and wood cutters. Many were guides when sport fishermen began to invade the Northland. The French preferred canoes, and so they became the boats of the frontier, their reputation enhanced years later by hundreds of camp programs.

The canvas and wooden canoes that followed those of birchbark were more practical for fishermen. Then aluminum brought a combination of lightness, toughness and freedom from maintenance. After aluminum came fiberglass and other compositions, even lighter for their strength. A boom in canoeing took place in the 1960s and 70s. Canoeing for the sake of canoeing was a growing sport. Cartopping, which had become popular in the 1930s, worked fine for canoes. At first the larger boats used for cartopping were made of wood and canvas, but aluminum took over most of that market.

A canoe poler is of a special breed, going upstream in a tortuous route a paddler could not follow. Taking advantage of the quiet edges and the current-parting boulders, he goes up past "haystacks" and standing waves that might frighten downstream travelers. Many an American sportsman has been astonished at such travel with a Canadian trout or salmon guide.

*Big 14-foot johnboat carries just about anything a
fisherman could need and goes fast with small motor.*

The true rowboat is often little more than a widened and shortened canoe with a squared stern, and when the first outboard motors came along they were clamped to that transom. But the johnboat was something else.

I don't even know why it's called a *johnboat,* but when I was a kid an Ozark gradeschooler told me he supposed it was because he had an uncle named John who made them. At first I considered this something of a joke, but I have since concluded it is as good an explanation as any I've heard. Some insist that it's *jonboat,* and while editors take great satisfaction in taking out the *h,* I am not sure they are justified.

There have been many flat statements as to who invented the johnboat. The craft is so simple in design that it was an obvious construction. Regardless of who created the first ones, *someone* coined the name at some specific time, however gradually the design developed.

It evidently got its start as the simplest of all the boats to build once cut planks were available. Simply a square-ender with planks for a bottom (lengthwise) and sides and bow cut to fit, the bow and stern turned up a little. Some were made with the bottom boards put on

"Float boats" as used on this Ozark river are refined versions of the wooden johnboats of half a century before.

crosswise, but the traditional Ozark johnboat had the planks going the long way. Experienced hill-country craftsmen could build one very quickly. The johnboat was the backbone of the Ozark "float trip." I understand that there were some 30-foot johnboats around 1900, their bottoms only 2 feet wide. That would resemble a pirogue, a longer, slender craft of the southern bayou. A typical "float boat" of the 1920s and later was about 20 feet long by 3 feet wide, and accommodated a guide and two fishermen.

The Ozarks of Missouri and Arkansas attracted smallmouth bass fishermen from across America for a sport that was at its peak when the world went to World War II. The hill-country rivers had quick "shoals," but even a heavy-laden johnboat could make it through them if the paddle man knew his business. Fishermen sat on folding chairs with camping gear between them. The guide paddled from the stern, his personal effects stashed in a burlap sack that served as a cushion on his board seat.

Those guides tended to wear bib overalls and dark felt hats in contrast to the clients, whose uniforms were almost universally khaki. Most of the fishing was baitcasting, the guide often carrying a stubby steel rod himself. Some lures were favored, many of them forgotten now. The Tom Thumb had its day, but perhaps most popular of all was the Peck Feather Minnow with propeller spinner and weighted head. Black and yellow were the favorite colors and most guides added a split strip of porkrind. Fly fishermen used either bugs or streamers, some with spinners ahead of wet flies.

Smallmouths darted out from alongside standing waves on the shoals and held against the willows in some of the bubbly runs. In the long, slow pools with chunk rock bottoms they were more cautious and casts had to be longer. Largemouths occupied some of the sloughs.

The float trip was an instant escape from a busy, swift-moving world. The landing disappeared around a bend as the fisherman adjusted his position in the canvas chair and made his first casts. Then until the end of the float it was woodsmoke smell in the river canyon, a view of cabins in small clearings and the song of coonhounds at evening camp.

At the float's end there were horses or mules to get the boats to a railway—later it was trucks—and the sportsmen rode back to their automobiles or Pullman cars to leave for their city offices. The guides went back to begin a new float, carrying their burlap sacks with a change of clothes and their paddles. These were shaped by hand, ranging from crude tools to those of jackknife artistry, but there was something about his own paddle that made a man an individual among his peers of bib overalls and felt hats.

Most of the smallmouth rivers are gone now, turned to silting, crooked grooves on the bottoms of great lakes above great dams with their power lines marching across the hills. The shoals have stilled and the hillside cabins are "structure" found by bass boat depthfinders. The clearings where the axe rang on summer evenings and the trails where the coonhound sang are long drowned, but there are more bass in the lakes than were ever in the rivers. It's changed, that's all.

But the johnboat didn't disappear. After the dams came it was used on the colder rivers below, where trout grew big. When aluminum gained popularity as a boat material the johnboat became a cartopper, back-country traveler, workboat and floater of rivers far from the Ozarks. In large sizes it became a bass boat. With a small outboard engine and smooth water it carried a big load fast, and it went well with oars and electric motors.

The names associated with the old wooden johnboats may not be

McKenzie drift boat has same silhouette as offshore dory and has become a favorite on trout and salmon rivers.

remembered long after the passing of those who fished in their boats. Jim Owens was the best-known float outfitter, with headquarters at Branson, Missouri. Charlie Barnes, guide and master riverman, also built johnboats, and several members of the Barnes family were well-known on the rivers in their day.

Seven hundred miles south of Jim Owens' headquarters, the pirogue developed in the Louisana bayou country. Like the johnboat, it was an offshoot of the canoe and first appeared as a dugout. Later it was made of other materials, and by the early 50s there were racing pirogues of oilcloth stretched over a frame of carefully glued wooden sections. The pirogue is perfect for following narrow boat trails through the swamps, and it comes in a wide range of sizes.

The first rubber boats, really liferafts, that served on fast rivers showed up after World War II, a byproduct of wartime aviation, and ran the really wild rivers along with the heavy wooden boats explorers had used before that time. The wooden boats were reinforced against rock and wave but the inflated rafts made it look easy. Dr. Russell Frazer, famous explorer and whitewater expert, viewed his first motion pictures of a rubber raft in the whitewater haystacks and shook his head a bit sadly: it was a new era. Frazer's wild rivers were suddenly tamed a little.

In the West, float fishing often involves wading as well as boating. The big rubber raft came into use after the war, and after the military surplus boats rotted, manufacturers were quick to make boats that held up even better against the rapids and the rocks.

The canoe has disadvantages as a guide boat on float trips. To run a river with a canoe and paddles it is necessary to outrun the current to gain steerage.

With a rubber raft the oarsman can hold back against the flow, easing his rig over the rough spots and giving his casters a chance to cover the water. Rigid frames hold the oarlocks. Rubber boats got bigger and tougher and were used more and more as tourist haulers on canyon rivers, but where the water was less violent the guides began to use medium-sized johnboats with oars. Rigid boats were easier to maneuver and worked better in the wind.

Then came the dory-type drift boat, with a silhouette almost exactly like the old banks dory and oars from 8 to 10 feet long. The craft is 14 to 16 feet long in most cases, takes the rough water easily and makes a perfect platform for fly casters, usually one in the bow and one in the stern, often with special yokes to lean against. The most popular material has been fiberglass although there are wooden and aluminum models. The true drift boat of this type (often called the *McKenzie boat*) became a status symbol for guides.

Another boat became popular as a drifter about 1970. The modern inflatable with a rigid bottom is a versatile design that can plane with outboard motors. They're made in America but in the larger sizes they originated in Europe. Rugged and virtually unsinkable, the modern inflatable may not be the best at any one job but it is a safe substitute in many kinds of fishing water.

The bass boat is a phenomenon of the boating industry: a design that caught on beyond the wildest dreams of the first builders, a remarkably efficient tool of the scientific bass fisherman and a status symbol in much of the South and Midwest. In the latter role it is an adjunct to the family car, sometimes displacing it, fitted with plush furniture and the latest in electronics. Stereo is sometimes an added attraction.

The bass boat started slowly and there was little indication that it

Probably the first "bass boat" was the Skeeter,
which made excellent use of the bow-mounted electric motor.

171

would bring a waiting line at the loan offices. No one can say exactly where it began, but I believe the first freshwater craft to be called a "bass boat" was the Skeeter, built in Texas. It was a slender flat-bottomed craft, partially decked over, that looked like an outsized duck boat. It went well with an electric motor in the bow. Some said it was a modified johnboat.

Next came boats with bow modifications borrowed from the "tri-hulls" and "cathedral hulls." These softened the ride a little and made the bow steady for a fisherman sitting or standing there. It was ideal for an electric motor mounted in front (before bow mounting, the electric never had reached its potential). By the early 70s some of the bass hulls were 18 feet long, weighed a thousand pounds and carried outboards up to 150 horsepower and occasionally more.

Bass fishermen wanted more speed, and since the deep impoundments were their main consideration the flat bottom was no longer deemed important. From this came the "pad boat" and then the vee hull, making the bass boat a rather dressy relative of the offshore

A forerunner of the modern outboard offshore fishing machine was Miss Print, *built from the ideas of Jim Martenhoff. The 23-footer had two fighting chairs installed in the bow.*

"fishing machine." It still floated low in the water for fishing convenience and was not made for heavy seas, but it could travel across a chop at high speed without too much pounding.

Fiberglass remained the most popular material although there were many light aluminum models, most patterned after the aluminum johnboat, but some had vee bows. The bass boat was efficient at its job, but it was a "bath tub" to saltwater fishermen who scoffed at much of its flossy gadgetry. They were busy saving for their own dream, the "fishing machine."

The "fishing machine" (which we call it for lack of a better term) came on later than most fishermen realize. Although the big offshore sportsfisherman had been well developed since the 1930s, the relatively inexpensive ocean-going outboard didn't really make it until the 1960s. The Boston Whaler started it all with its strange bottom and extreme buoyancy, making a debut that set off innumerable multiple-bottom designs. The Whaler went where no little boat had dared go.

I think Jim Martenhoff did more than anyone else to develop the offshore fishing machine, and the Allied Angler boat introduced at the Miami Boat Show in 1965 was the first to be called "fishing machine" as far as I know. The concept was a bit different from that of the first Whalers, the fishing machine following more conventional bottom lines, having considerable freeboard and using more interior space.

Martenhoff, offshore racer, boating writer and marine consultant, had gone all-out in *Miss Print*, a 23-footer intended for offshore use and carrying two big outboards. As he says:

"There were two fighting chairs forward. The theory was to troll normally (if you trolled) but if you got a hookup you swung the boat and chair around and fought the fish bows-on—ahead of the boat. That way you could maneuver easily, even in a sea. The boat was meant for anything from bonefish to blue marlin. She caught plenty of bonefish, too, poled easily from the bow, and you can see in one of the photos how little water she drew—just a few inches."

On one variation of *Miss Print*, the bow deck was extended aft on each side of the console, all the way to the transom. The self-bailing cockpit was, in effect, a well deck.

These big, fast outboards didn't come cheap, but compared to the cost of a 40-foot offshore sportsfisherman it was chickenfeed. Saltwater fishermen who had languished in bays and tidal rivers now found they could be their own skippers and go out to the blue water. Like the bass boat, and at about the same time, the "fishing machine" redesigned a corner of the boating industry.

Jim Martenhoff's original designs had been built as all-around saltwater boats but the rigs became more specialized very quickly. The offshore fishermen went for more vee in the bottoms and didn't worry about poling. The flats, bay and back-country fishermen went for slightly smaller boats with emphasis on poling and electric motor use. They went to the poling platform, set above the motor, and took pride in cockpits that had nothing to snag a line or trip an excited fisherman. The saltwater outboard brought big fish to the man of average income, and things would never be the same.

The fishing machine and the bass boat looked very different and the owner of one might scorn the other, but in their social significance they were brothers under the hull: efficient, fast and comfortable. The outboard motor made them possible.

The outboard was a slow bloomer. Such an engine had to be remarkably efficient for its weight or it couldn't serve as a "rowboat motor." There were attempts at steam-driven outboards, believed to

Bonefisherman operates from completely equipped flats boat with guide on poling platform.

have started in Europe; then came electric motors driven by storage batteries, a far cry from the modern trolling gadget. William Steinway, the piano man, together with Gottfried Daimler, "father of the gasoline engine," introduced a gasoline engine for boats at the Chicago World's Fair in 1893.

Cameron Waterman apparently started the term *outboard* in 1907, and his concern built an outboard motor called the Waterman Porto from 1906 through 1915, selling some 30,000 of them.

Ole Evinrude built his first motor in 1907 in Milwaukee and Ole's wife, Bess, wrote an advertisement with the advice, *Throw Away the Oars*. During those early years it was a good idea to keep the oars around, but the slogan caught on and so did the single-cylinder motor, developing one-half horsepower while achieving about 1000 RPM. Evinrude's engine had the same general configuration as its modern descendants and subsequent progress was uninterrupted.

The flywheel magneto was designed in 1914 and for a time the battery disappeared. The motors used before World War I were too heavy, too noisy and not powerful enough, but aluminum brought light weight. Remote controls were installed by Elto in 1926 and hoods began muffling the constantly more powerful engines in 1934. There had been considerable work on gearshifts but it was 1949 before they were introduced on commercial models. They civilized the beast, and it was no longer necessary to take aim before pulling the starter rope.

Until about 1950 the outboard market had been divided rather sharply. The fishermen wanted light, small engines that could be clamped to rowboats and carried in their cars. The "boaters" and racers wanted big, fast engines that tended to be a bit cranky for such things as trolling, or even much idling. But in the early 50s a number of American builders came forth with more tractable monsters—a prelude to the fishing machine and the bass boat.

With modern design and metallurgy, a motor of up to 20 horsepower was fairly portable and fit in a car trunk. Rental boats over most of the country were made to handle them. Trailer boating began to boom.

By the 70s the big outboard had come into its own as a special kind of powerplant. It was mostly outside the boat, an advantage in fire safety, and it didn't take up fishing room inside. For its weight, its power was awesome. While no one was going to carry a 200-horse outboard under his arm, the power-per-pound had made fishing a new game. A 100-mile, one-day trip from dock to fishing grounds was no longer a pioneering expedition. In fact, the fast outboards were putting a new look on fish management. People got everywhere too fast.

By 1981 there was special emphasis on outboard motors for the larger offshore cruisers. They were meant to serve the purpose of the "outdrive," an inboard engine with a tilting outboard-type propeller and lower unit.

No one made too much speed with the belly boat, floater bubble or tube float, whatever you want to call it. It must have started around 1920 because prior to that time innertubes were too skinny to make very good floats. At any rate, the tube float was common in the 30s. Most of those were homemade, simply some sort of saddle rigged for an inflated truck tube. The "saddle," generally made of canvas, allowed the fisherman to drift over water that was too deep to wade. Then came suspenders or galluses to hold the float up while its operator walked, presenting a rather unusual appearance, especially if he had homemade paddles on his legs.

Smallest of the modern "small-water" boats is the floater bubble or belly boat, which began with innertubes, probably in the 1920s.

176

I believe most of the earlier ones were used in the Midwest and northern Midwest and that the users were mainly bass fishermen who carried them to the smaller lakes and creeks, where they could be used in grassy waters where a boat wasn't much help.

The first commercial models were canvas covers, bought with or without the innertube, with snap or zipper pockets for small items of equipment. Half a century after the first truck tubes went to sea, the commercial floats could be had in either rigid or inflatable plastic and were found on cold trout lakes of the West as well as weedy sloughs in the South. The fastest locomotion was provided by swim fins with which the floater could push himself backwards, but if he didn't want his feet encumbered he could use little hand paddles.

Some of the modern floats even have tenders and it is not unusual to see a fly fisherman slipping along a sheltered shoreline, towing behind him another float that might carry beer, sandwiches and a portable radio.

The opposite extreme in angling flotation is the current offshore sportsfisherman, usually a day cruiser and probably less than 40 feet long, although some are live-aboard yachts. The common denominators are modern fighting chairs, flying bridge (and possibly a third level or tuna tower), metal outriggers and electronic equipment for navigation and fish finding. Diesel power was growing in popularity in the 60s and 70s.

Another type of craft, often used for charter, is a good-sized open inboard for relatively short runs. Long called a "tarpon boat" in the South, on the northern Atlantic coast a very similar rig has been called a "bass boat" (meaning striped bass rather than black bass). Both are still used today, although I believe they were more common in the 1950s.

Continuing his love affair with his car, the fisherman of 1980 was likely to depend on a trailer to get his boat to water. Fuel problems were forcing him toward lighter boats to some extent.

CHAPTER ELEVEN

KEEPING SCORE

Izaak Walton wouldn't have approved but fishermen have a habit of keeping score. Contemplative anglers might look the other way but it has been competition that developed tackle and fishing methods and has aided research.

The simple case is that competition leads to organization and organization is the key to progress. Fishing clubs tend to compete and become larger organizations that are international forces for fish management and conservation in general.

Angling competition falls into three rough classifications: casting, head-to-head fishing tournaments and long-term record keeping.

Casting, now overshadowed by actual fishing contests, has been a measurement of skill for well over 100 years, predating reliable big-fish records. The casters, minor sports heroes at one time, developed our tackle.

When American rodmakers began to rival English manufacturers in quality they used casting tournaments for advertising, and their equipment beat the English. There was nothing wrong with the American rods, of course, but it may be that American casters had

*Tournament casting was instrumental in developing
modern tackle. This distance fly caster coils his running line
on a canvas and it is tended by a "gillie" (right).*

another advantage: perhaps they had taken it more seriously and were better prepared. They were looking for markets.

The news media have never quite learned how to handle sport fishing. For the most part they now departmentalize it with hunting, accepting the fact that it is not a truly general interest subject. Newspaper editors have found that the "outdoor" readers will find it, no matter how deeply buried in the sports section. Radio and television executives have had a more difficult time. Fifteen minutes of fishing on radio or television means that there will be 15 minutes less of other programs. Their constant quest is for something that will appeal to the entire public.

Ever since the first casting contests there have been efforts at making fishing a general interest subject. When the *Spirit of the Times* first ran fishing material (subordinate to horse racing) it was obviously not expected to appeal to anyone but anglers or prospective anglers. Casting contests prompted efforts at appealing to the general public. Of course fishing was not a spectator sport that would compete with baseball, but for that matter golf was not considered much of a spectator sport at first, and the record shows that it became a crowd attractor.

Public attitude toward angling in the media is well exemplified by the efforts of national television in the 60s. The idea of the "outdoor show" was kicked around by creative television minds and constantly related back to spectator sports. The public watched athletics on TV, but most of the appeal came through the process of deciding a winner and a loser. Competition between an angler and a fish was not enough, the programmers decided. There had to be a human winner and a human loser if the public was to be entertained.

So the first of the big-time television outdoor shows featured far-out and far-fetched fishing "contests," which appeared to have all the true competition of professional wrestling with something less in showmanship. Never mind that the competitors were truly fine anglers. No matter where they went there was the hushed commentary associated with golf tournaments, and even huge scoreboards recording the points made by some outdoor personality as he strove to catch more 10-inch trout or more 100-pound tarpon than his equally famous "adversary."

All of this life-and-death struggle was a mite pallid for serious fishermen, although it may have appealed to some "general public" viewers. At any rate, crappie fishing showed no sign of usurping prime time from the World Series.

Another solution was the use of prominent athletic figures. Most of the world's best anglers, it developed, weren't the most dramatic actors anyway and were likely to produce, "Oh boy!" or other less than deathless prose as a 7-foot sailfish tailwalked. If they memorized their lines it was likely to sound that way.

The halfbacks and center fielders, it developed, weren't always the best actors either and sometimes they didn't know whether the reel went above or below the rod. Nevertheless, the names were an attraction. The best of those shows have involved an actor-expert who conveys a bit of how-to information to an athletic personality.

There have been some fortunate shows that involved famous personalities who happened to be masters at some phase of the sport. Bing Crosby, for example, was a serious fisherman who showed no sign of stage fright before a camera. Baseball's Ted Williams came across as a fine angler. These shows took the place of the staged

Two national casting champions of not so long ago were Joan Salvato and the late Jon Tarantino, shown here in a casting exhibition.

contests for productions such as ABC's *American Sportsman,* but competition returned in a completely different form later on.

When big bass tournaments and other fishing contests managed to establish their own heroes, some of them began their own television shows and some of them were pleasant personalities. They sold fishing tackle and gave angling information. There were a few exceptions, such as the Gadabout Gaddis fishing program. Gaddis didn't make his reputation in contests; he was simply a good fisherman with an airplane and an interesting flow of comment.

All of this coverage of fishing, on television and radio as well as in newspapers, had settled into a niche of specialized watchers, listeners and readers. The audience is hardly general, and certainly competitive casting is a mystery for almost all of the general public and most fishermen. Steve Rajeff, a national casting champion, is a hero to those who follow the games even casually, but his public image is probably somewhere behind that of a utility fielder for the Boston Red Sox.

These thoughts about publicity are an introduction to the history of competition in fishing, the most visible facet of the "contemplative" sport.

Casting competition definitely sold fishing tackle in the 19th century, but in the late 20th the casting games seemed to have lost much of their direct influence on the market. Advertising of the 1980s does not tout the fact that a certain make of rod won a national casting event any more than an Oldsmobile ad stresses wins by that car in stock racing. As in the case of the automobile that wins, competition tackle is undoubtedly customized, if not built for competition from the ground up.

Nevertheless, tackle development very often begins on the casting platform—a place where results are measurable. No backyard experiment can equal the achievement of actually winning distance or accuracy events. Nearly all of the innovations in casting method are competition born. Once they are adopted by fishermen it sometimes seems ridiculous that such simple tactics had to be discovered in competition.

Competitive casting began in the 1860s along with baseball. (Basketball hadn't been worked out yet and football was a sort of collegiate gang fight). The great casters of the early days were almost all fishing tackle makers, sporting goods dealers, outdoor writers or fisheries biologists.

Apparently they went into casting from these other occupations, rather than the other way around. The same fields are likely to produce competitive casters today, but the casting games are not so exclusively owned by such professionals. Many top casters have turned professional and have held their own professional competitions.

Cliff Netherton, former president of the American Casting Association, in writing a history of the games credited Fred Mather as compiling the first detailed set of rules for tournament casting. They were used at the Coney Island, Brighton Beach Tournament in 1881. Mather became secretary of the National Rod and Reel Association in 1882. As a fish culturist he was a founder of the American Fisheries Society in 1871. He held several important national posts in fish management and was the recipient of those famous brown trout eggs sent from Germany in 1883. Like most casters of the time, he wrote about fishing. Mather became director of a private fish hatchery in 1899.

From the very earliest accounts of competitive casting it seems that Reuben Wood was a standout, certainly the most consistent winner, and at the time the term "unbeatable" may have applied to him. Because the equipment was very different from today's, the figures may not mean much except to indicate progress. In 1873 Wood won a tournament with a flycast of 65 feet. In 1881 he cast a salmon fly 110 feet and was throwing the trout fly past the 80-foot mark. As a sporting goods dealer, he invented some fishing gear.

Evidently the rules were roughly similar to modern ones. The salmon fly event involves a two-handed rod while the trout fly is cast with one hand. It appears that line "shooting" as done by modern fly casters was not well developed and the early lines simply weren't well adapted to it. Emphasis was on fly casting since the modern plug casting method wasn't developed until after 1900; remember that Henshall didn't approve of short rods. Bass fishing with artificial casting lures was a long time coming.

I don't find much on early competitive surf casting, despite the New England striped bass clubs, which were at their peak while casting tournaments were getting started. Surf fishermen used natural baits, not conducive to extremely hard throwing, but great things were claimed for their distance and accuracy. Anyway, the casting games were developed mainly for lighter tackle as used in fresh water. Even today, although surf casting rules are part of the American Casting Association, such events are not as prominent as the others.

Going back to 1882, we find that Harry Pritchard, an Englishman who was at that time in the tackle business in New York, won a casting tournament with a roll cast of 91 feet. Only a few years earlier 70 feet would have won most tourneys.

It was logical that rollcasting came from England. It is done well with the long rods the British preferred, and still prefer to some extent. Most American fishermen use it only for the purpose of picking up line to be cast by a more conventional method, or for use in close quarters with no room for a backcast. However, the roll cast, when properly developed, will give distances even greater than

Small Meek Number 2 reel, using lightweight arbor,
is dwarfed by Shakespeare Lurecast (left) and
Langley Target. Tournament casters sometimes used
Meeks long after more modern reels were available.

Pritchard threw. I suspect it has reached its peak with the West Coast steelheaders, using leadcore or other very heavy fly lines and monofilament shooting lines. They learned the roll through necessity, often having to cast with their backs to banks or bushes.

A list of early tournament fly casters reads like a compilation of the fishing famous. Seth Green (1817-1888) was good and so was Robert B. Roosevelt, once president of the American Fisheries Society. Roosevelt won a fly casting tournament in 1864 by casting 63 feet with a cedar rod. Using his left hand, he got 57 feet. A contemporary competitor of his was Charles Hallock, publisher of *Forest and Stream*. Willis Barnum, sporting goods dealer and resort operator, was a winner in the 1880s. Charles Mowry, publisher of *Sporting Goods Gazette,* came on a little later. Considerably later, Edward Ringwood Hewitt, better known as an all-around authority on trout and salmon, was a winning tournament performer.

When split bamboo took over the fly rod business some of the regular winners in America and abroad were rod manufacturers themselves. Near the end of the century the Leonard rods set records, and among the best known of the performers were Hiram Hawes, Reuben Leonard and Ed Mills. By 1900 distances had increased considerably. Much later the tournaments gave a boost to Winston and Powell bamboo rods.

Today there is a difference in the association of business and platform competition: in those days tackle makers seemed to head for the tournaments; now the casting champions gravitate toward tackle business.

When American bamboo rod builders took to the tournaments to prove their quality, it developed that the Americans had better casting tools than the British. While the British had led in fly fishing techniques up until late in the 19th century, their methods of fishing were somewhat different. For one thing, their extremely long rods lacked the firepower of athletically wielded shorter sticks. The English didn't do much long casting for trout. Brown trout in the meadow streams were different targets than rainbows on roaring mountain rivers— and the steelhead placed a premium on distance. The British didn't go in for much long casting except for Atlantic salmon, and there they went for big two-handed rods.

The American bamboo fly rod builders became heroes of the tackle

*Bob Budd, long-time winner in casting tournaments,
shows baitcasting form during a tournament
of the 1950s.*

business and their names have lasted for more than a hundred years. There isn't that much made of the old British rods, according to collectors, and no British name has the connotation of Leonard or Payne. At the same time, British workmanship has been prized in fly reels and connoisseurs give them snob appeal over American makes. There is no doubt of their fine workmanship. We can only say that American factory reels are adequate, rugged and less expensive.

Some developments have come directly from the casting platform. One is the fly caster's double haul, a device for adding line speed, which is converted into casting distance.

The single haul, much simpler to learn, came first. In executing the single haul, the caster starts the maneuver on the fishing cast, after the line is beginning to straighten on his backcast. As the rod comes forward, the line-tending hand (left hand for righthanded casters) pulls line briskly through the guides and then releases it as the forward cast is terminated.

The double haul requires a bit of special timing and practice. In executing it, additional line is fed through the guides as the backcast is under way. Then there is a forward haul as the rod tip heads toward the target and thus more speed is gained as the line is released, so considerable line is shot through the guides. Today, all distance events requiring one-hand rods are won with the double haul. Most fishermen using heavy outfits execute the move as a routine method.

Most of the very earliest casting tournaments were handled by general fishing clubs. The American Casting Association, as it is now called, began in 1906 as the National Association of Angling Clubs.

At about that time the snap cast used in baitcasting (and later spinning) accuracy events got its start. When throwing artificial plugs it was unnecessary to deliver with an easy sweep. The tournament caster's delivery of a baitcasting plug with a short, flexible rod enabled him to look over the rod tip, hold it out in front and keep it in view through most of the operation. The accuracy cast is delivered hard and its flat trajectory minimizes misjudgment and wind effects. Some tournament people have used the simple instruction, *Throw hard and thumb hard,* in describing their style. This may be an over-simplification, but champions certainly don't lob their casts. The short tournament casting rod was introduced to competition by Lloyd Tooley and Tilden Robb in 1905.

While distance competition with fly rods never strayed far from usable tackle, there was an offshoot in the distance baitcasting events, where there was a premium upon mechanical perfection and ultra-light lines. Reels became very narrow-spooled mechanical marvels, reducing friction to almost nothing and depending upon carefully concocted lubricants. A distance caster might carry a whole chest of bottles containing oil mixtures for every reel and every weather condition. Most baitcasting distance events have not employed practical fishing tackle and the distances achieved make poor comparison with what a good fisherman can do with his bass rod.

The casting people have repeatedly arranged special events for practical fishing gear and are entitled to enjoy a little specialized instrumentation with attendant custom engineering. Nevertheless, a constant theme of casters' meetings is the problem of "getting the fishermen interested." Although most competitors are also practical anglers, they have long been aware that the casting phase of their sport is highly specialized and often frightening to anglers.

Some of the twentieth century champions should be recognized, partly because of the new equipment they brought with them.

Marvin Hedge of Oregon (1896-1969) set a world record in the distance fly event at St. Louis in 1934. There is no doubt he was one of the greatest casters of all but some of his expertise came from rod and line design. Like many great distance champions to come later, Hedge spliced his own tapers, one factor in a highly technical phase of the game. The micrometer was an effective ally of muscle and timing.

Distance fly casting stretched out in 1946 when two well-known competitors came up with monofilament running (shooting) line. The two, both of whom have been consistent winners, were Jim Green and Phil Miraville. Up to that time the running line had been silk. Monofilament was coming into its own for the new spinning tackle, and with its slick surface and minimum diameter Green won the fly distance event at a national tournament in Indianapolis.

Green and Miraville were members of the Golden Gate Casting Club of San Francisco, which has produced a large share of the national champions. Green, a rod designer, is a specialist in fly casting and has promoted accuracy events employing practical fishing tackle. Miraville has been one of the most successful casting instructors in the game.

Myron Gregory, another West Coast caster-fisherman, worked out

Winners pose before marlin caught off Cape Hatteras during a tournament. Competition fostered offshore expertise in 1980.

a formula for classification of fly lines and rods. When line size was designated by letter there was little uniformity between manufacturers, and tackle shoppers were handicapped. The number designation of lines classified them by weight and it was then possible for a rodmaker to designate exactly the lines his product would work with.

Bob Budd rates special attention as a competitive caster. He began in the 30s and won the Grand All Around championship in 1947. An Indianian, Budd was not only a casting perfectionist but a master mechanic of fishing tackle. He built his own bamboo rods and was one of the first competitors to use fiberglass. When he designed a ball bearing distance reel he and his grandson, Terry Schneider, dominated that division for some time. Budd took a closed-face spinning reel, developed a fingering device for it, and won accuracy events with it. As a coach he had impeccable credentials. His daughter Mollie Light, his grandson and his step-grandson, Devin Light, also won national championships.

Budd was a muscular 145 pounds and took great delight in designing distance lines and rods to defeat much bigger men in the salmon fly distance event, a competition alleged to require considerable beef. He preached that his success was due to equipment design, but the fact is there was superb coordination and not a little power in Budd's makeup. Outside the game he was not the best-known of casting champions but his career exemplifies the game's contribution to fishing.

Although an occasional fisherman scoffs at tournament casters and wonders if they ever go fishing, the accomplishments of tournament people on stream, lake and sea have become legendary. The stories are endless, such as the one of the tarpon guide on the Florida Keys who took Ben Hardesty of Shakespeare as a client without knowing he was a casting champion. The guide staked out near a channel and told Hardesty to cast to the edge of it. Hardesty obediently did this for a while. No tarpon.

The guide was in a bad humor that day and wished he had someone who could cast far out into the channel.

"Could you throw it way out there?" the guide finally grunted petulantly. Hardesty did and the guide later reported: "The sun went down and the moon came up and the damned line was still going!"

Champions of the 30s included Tony Accetta and Fred Arbogast, names that have survived in connection with tackle developments.

Cliff Netherton picks out the names of all-time champions: Hardy (of British tackle), Ritz (Charles Ritz, French caster and author-promoter of fly fishing), and Leonard, Hawes, Mills, Powell, Stoner, Merrick and Granger, all concerned with fly rod manufacture.

Of the most recent champions, Jon Tarantino was among the best known. Currently, the top winners include Steve Rajeff, who became national all-around champion for the ninth straight year in 1980, his brother Tim Rajeff, Chris Korich and Zack Willson. Of course many winners are not included, most of them famous within the casting fraternity but little known among anglers in general. Steve Rajeff had been world champion six times by 1980, when he lost to West German Walter Pfandl.

Casting is a game of supreme coordination and fine mechanisms, but secrets of reel construction, fly-line tapers and weight and rod dimensions are poorly kept and any ardent beginner should soon be able to put together a usable kit.

Some of the distances acquired in national competition are surprising to non-competitive casters. For example, it takes nearly 200 feet to win a fly distance event (single hand); two-handed fly distance is likely to be more than 250 feet. The anglers fly distance event uses true fishing tackle and can get as much as 170 feet. With specialized gear the one-ounce plug may go more than 500 feet. To be classified in the championship division of surf casting, a competitor must throw more than 500 feet in the 4-ounce unrestricted game.

At times, leading casters have been technicians whose gear was, temporarily at least, hard to duplicate. This has scared off a few potential competitors. The complaint most frequently heard is that the casting games do not apply to practical fishing, but Skish and other practical events have employed stock fishing equipment. It is true that the same names appear repeatedly in the list of winners, but the fact that several members of the same family can be national champions indicates that dedication is an ingredient that surpasses any vagrant quality of muscle or knowledge.

Anyway, fishing needs the casting games and casting clubs.

Competition has furnished some of the best and worst in sport angling. Many a civic leader who has innocently accepted a post on the committee of a local fishing contest has been appalled at the perfidy of his fellow man.

Citizens who would be horrified at the suggestion of shoplifting or

*Organized record keeping really began when
Michael Lerner (shown here with swordfish taken at
Cape Breton, Nova Scotia in 1941) helped organize and
finance the IGFA.*

embezzlement will go to great lengths to win a fishing contest by trickery, sometimes when the prize is only a trophy. A large percentage of prize entries are found to contain lead sinkers or stones. Such shenanigans are not restricted to the peasantry. There is the offshore specimen with a large squid in its body cavity, having somehow been jammed in so as to miss the stomach. Frozen fish may be clumsily thawed out for entry in the head-to-head competition. There is the "stakeout" fish held in a livebox pending the opening of the one-day freshwater tournament.

But competitive record keeping and organized club fishing have contributed most to scientific research. Fishing regulations have depended greatly upon tournament findings. "Organized" fishing with international tackle requirements has existed for only 40 years. Before that, tackle specifications were a matter for the individual club.

The International Game Fishing Association (IGFA), the leader in salt water, was organized in 1940 and is now almost universally recognized for both salt and freshwater records—but that was a long time in coming.

The Catalina Tuna Club and the Izaak Walton Tarpon Club were among the best known of the early record keepers and they gave buttons for exceptional catches. Similar programs were started by dozens of fishing organizations in the early 1900s. *Field & Stream* put freshwater fishing records on a national basis with an annual contest, beginning their program in 1910. It did not involve many tackle restrictions, and since there was no money involved, entries were rather simply made.

The IGFA was the handiwork of Michael Lerner, who financed it for a generation. Lerner and the others who were in at the beginning were deep-water fishermen and the early rules were centered around offshore boats and blue water tackle. In 1940 this was largely a rich man's sport but the purposes of the IGFA were unselfish. Lerner was interested in big ocean fish, but catching them was only part of it; he was concerned with scientific study.

The idea began to work when Lerner conducted a fishing expedition to Australia in conjunction with the American Museum of Natural History in New York and learned that the British Tunny Club had considered an international organization. At the organizational meeting in 1939 were Dr. William King Gregory of the Museum, who was a member of the New Zealand-Australia expedition; Francesca LaMonte, associate curator of fishes at the museum; Lerner and Van Campen Heilner, writer and well-known saltwater angler. Gregory became the first president and Miss LaMonte worked with the organization in a scientific capacity until her retirement in 1978.

From its beginning the IGFA attracted a list of celebrities. Ernest Hemingway and Philip Wylie were both successful writers in other fields but prone to stick considerable offshore fishing into their work. Wylie was a regular in the *Saturday Evening Post* with a series of "Crunch and Des" stories about fictional characters who operated a charter boat in Florida. Their adventures became so popular with outdoor readers that it was sometimes difficult to separate Wylie from his brainchildren. He was, however, a proficient angler in his own right.

Lerner designed and demonstrated survival fishing equipment for servicemen during World War II, traveling wherever such services were needed. He provided the IGFA with quarters in Miami when the museum became crowded.

William Carpenter, a pioneer bluefin tuna angler, became president of the IGFA in 1960 and moved the headquarters to Fort Lauderdale, Florida. Elwood K. Harry, a widely traveled saltwater fisherman and vice president since 1962, suggested in the early 70s that the organization be opened to private memberships and secure its funding in that way. Harry became president in 1975. The program of individual membership got under way in 1973, and from the record-keeping angle, it was time for some changes.

The entire operation had been keyed to offshore fishing. Some light tackle inshore experts complained that there was no place for them. For example, the rules prohibited the multiple hooks used in plug-casting—fair enough for offshore trolling or "baiting" but bad news for a fellow using bass tackle who landed a 150-pound tarpon on 18-pound line to find that his catch was ineligible, whereas a man using single-hooked dead bait on the bottom could make the record book.

Ninety percent of the newer saltwater anglers, no matter how proficient or ethical, had no idea of what the IGFA really was. Most of them felt it was simply a perpetual contest, had no idea how it was funded and had never heard of its scientific contributions. Rules to fit new fishing methods as well as the offshore operations might not be terribly complicated once set up, but the process of doing so ran into some sticky problems. For example, take the double line.

For offshore trolling a long section of double line above the leader was quite logical. When some of the new inshore rule lawyers found out about it they chortled happily, went out and hooked some record fish with little more than the double line out. Such things were changed in short order but it was a hectic time.

Field & Stream was the best freshwater record keeper known and had the most complete listing. In 1978 *Field & Stream* turned the freshwater book over to the IGFA. The Salt Water Fly Rodders of

No marlin of this size can be called routine but
this tournament fish had plenty of competition.
In some tournaments such fish are weighed while sailfish are
counted and released.

195

America, who had kept records for some 15 years in a field almost unknown prior to that, gave their records to the IGFA, and so did the International Spin Fishing Association. Spinning had been so completely new and so completely different 30 years before that it was logical to keep separate records, but the turning spools and stationary spools were no longer operating in different social circles and line test became enough of a denominator.

The IGFA has representatives in more than 65 countries and provinces and has been a leader in fish management matters. Sport fishing has supplied specimens for study that could not be managed otherwise and the release concept has made possible worldwide tagging, both efforts that have produced new concepts about fish supply and migration.

Today, no one knows how many fishing clubs there are. The big offshore organizations are well documented but there are few communities that do not have some sort of organized fishing group, and no one knows how many contests there are annually. A large share of the clubs surface when fish management becomes a question, as in the proposal for a 200-mile coastal limit for U.S. fishing regulations. Clubs have an enormous influence in legislative matters.

Contests and tournaments have produced rod and reel feats that would have been thought impossible only a few years ago. In the 50s, when fly fishermen began to score regularly on really large tarpon, an inland fly expert watched his first explosive strike end in a broken leader and nodded sagely.

"I knew that fly business on tarpon was a batch of lies," he said.

Good reels and rods that truly match a line or leader have helped, but much of the big-fish catching is a result of knowledge of methods and of the fish itself. It developed that shark tackle wasn't needed for tarpon and the 1,000-pound "barrier" for rod and reel catches has dissolved. While careful operators use 6-pound line on fish once considered targets for nothing less than 80-pound test, others go for giants with any weight of tackle. Today, it is not unusual to see pickup trucks with mounted fighting chairs, ready to back up to the surf for shark fishing.

Some of the records seem to defy reason. For example, the fly rod is generally considered a tool for fish that fight near the surface but Bart Foth caught a 356-pound jewfish at Islamorada, Florida, in 1967 using

Ray Scott (with microphone), father of the bass tournaments, poses with a winner. (From the BASS collection)

a 12-pound tippet. Of course, the modern saltwater fighting rod for use with flies has little resemblance to the better-known trout tackle. Saltwater fish don't often take imitations of insects but it's still called fly fishing.

Lee Wulff caught a 148-pound striped marlin on a fly using a 12-pound tippet, and Stuart Apte's Pacific sailfish, also on a 12-pound tippet, weighed 136 pounds. At present, the fly rod record is a 182-pound tarpon caught by Billy Pate at Homosassa Springs, Florida—the place where they say someone will eventually break the 200-pound barrier with 15-pound leader.

Among the biggest rod and reel catches is Alfred C. Glassell's 1560-pound black marlin from Cabo Blanco, Peru in 1953. Alfred Dean caught a white shark weighing 2664 pounds in South Australia (1959). When we realize that such a creature is as heavy as a very large draft horse the feat takes on extra color.

Six-pound line, easily snapped with your fingers, landed a 244-pound black marlin off Panama for Edwin D. Kennedy. Many other records may have been just as hard to set but these big figures are especially impressive.

Freshwater records, not nearly so involved with method and line test, have been changing more slowly. The "biggest record of all" is George W. Perry's largemouth bass from Montgomery Lake, Georgia, back in 1932. It weighed 22 pounds, 4 ounces, and bass promoters swear that a bigger fish would be worth a million dollars in prizes and promotions. Other records indicate Perry's giant should have come from Florida but it simply didn't. After the Florida bass was installed in California, Ray Easley caught a 21 pound, 3.2 ounce fish at Lake Casitas near Los Angeles. A million-dollar bass seems possible.

The black bass tournament of today began as what appeared a foolhardy enterprise of Ray Scott, founder of the Bass Anglers Sportsman's Society. It changed sport fishing completely, made millionaires, and some say it saved the small boat industry. It has created a new jargon almost as distinctive as CB radio and has caused English professors to adopt a hillbilly dialect as part of the atmosphere. While trout anglers describe their catches as "gleaming shards of burnished color," the bass contestant insists he fishes for "them hawgs" and that he hopes to catch some "sows." While trout fishing authorship tends towards Latin terms and moody rhetoric, many of the *bassin'* clan abhor such effete approaches and write carefully to avoid being accused of literacy.

All of this paradox has nothing to do with the highly technical approach of the bass tournament winner, who knows more about bass and catches more bass than all of the "experts" who went before. In bass fishing, the old-timer is generally an over-aged novice.

Scott, an Alabama insurance man, started the Bass Anglers Sportsman's Society in 1968. Bass fishing was getting scientific and Scott thought the local masters would pay entry fees to compete with experts from other areas, so he set up a tournament in Arkansas. All of this seemed a bit wild to most observers but the stage had been set.

The bass boat was being developed, together with the electric motor and the compact depth finder. Most important, the fishermen were learning to operate successfully on the big impoundments, especially in the South. They were learning that bass could be caught at considerable depth and were present even after the new lake's characteristic boom had subsided. And the plastic worm was appearing as the most effective lure ever developed.

For the week-end "cast-for-cash" angler the tournament trail (the first tournament led to a series of them) was an opportunity to use fast, colorful boats with appealing gadgetry and to wear clothing decorated with all sorts of patches advertising fishing lures, outboard motors and the wearer's home club. Jumpsuits became a popular uniform and the competitor and his imitators took on an appearance hauntingly resembling a stock car race driver.

Tournament bass fishing is not exactly a spectator sport since the widely scattered competitors are hard to watch, but the weigh-ins attract festive crowds and there are exhibits such as new boats and motors. After the first year or two the weigh-in crowds began to know the famous competitors such as Roland Martin and Bill Dance and studied the enormous scoreboard with interest.

Super-salesman Ray Scott presided at the microphone, big-hatted and homey, not faking his Alabama accent but not curbing it either. Ten years after that first tournament BASS membership had grown into the hundreds of thousands. It was astonishing to note that ladies of the tournament neighborhoods brought him gourmet dishes (delivered at weigh-in) and he had attained a celebrity status roughly equivalent to a top-notch country singer. In the busy background was

Roland Martin, shown here early in his tournament career,
was a leader of the new school of scientific bass fishing.

a bright publicity man named Bob Cobb, whose press releases were written with friendly urgency.

Of course there was a crowd of imitators, some of them successful although never as well known as Scott. There were dozens of other impresarios who promoted clubs and tournaments of various sizes, not to compete with BASS but simply to apply a community promotion and have some fun.

The news media have never known what to do with bass tournaments. Many outdoor editors disapprove of "cast-for-cash." Some communities are a little aghast at the presence of 200 high-speed bass boats on a weekend. But the bass tournament has boomed boating and resort tackle businesses, and the attendant seminars and tournament pressure have led to a practical knowledge of bass fishing never before approached. It is a new sport with an old fish.

At first there was the spectre of experts catching too many bass, even though the catch was given to charitable institutions. Then came the release program in which the fish were brought to weigh-in, handled in plastic bags and released. Studies showed the survival rate was excellent. BASS then leaped into the forefront of a series of fish conservation causes with money and members. The contemplative fisherman could say he didn't like the competition business, but he was a little short on good reasons.

Scott became a favorite speaker at all sorts of anglers' meetings. After a dinner with trout anglers he would be the naive country boy who was considering "getting myself some rubber pants and trying this business." The trout fisherman loved it.

He pushed measures to make the invasion by his tournament circus as painless as possible. BASS restricted the power of motors used in tournaments and did away with the racing start in which all competitors scratched off with the gun; now they leave the dock at intervals. For a time it appeared the whole thing was turning into a boat race; most of the competitors had certain spots they wished to fish and wanted to get there first.

Of course there is the fellow who pretends to have trouble with his engine. During his practice runs he'll locate bass within a hundred yards of the starting dock and after the crowd leaves he has those fish to himself.

Supervision of a BASS tournament is almost foolproof. Each boat contains two competitors who keep a watch on each other. The combinations change regularly and the competitors trade places in the boat. Legal limits are observed, winners being decided by weight, and BASS has set its own size limit, even where there are none at the site of the tournaments.

Izaak Walton may whirl in his grave but he would have a hard time finding fault.

When the BASS tournament season begins in a Florida winter, sunrise comes late. A check-in dock for competitors is the end of a long line of powerful bass boats, the running lights winking as their operators move about in preparation. At that time the usually boisterous bassing crowd is a bit hushed in concentration upon the day's start. As the boats are checked for hidden pre-start catches (all have aerated live wells), the long line of boats stretches from the dock lights into darkness. At weigh-in the atmosphere will be different and noisy, a crowd gathering around the scales and the big mobile aquarium where the fish are temporarily quartered until they can be released.

Some of the bassmen are full-time competitors, representing tackle companies or boating concerns, and as the season wears on some of them are haggard from hard work and early rising. They compete not only in BASS tourneys but many others and they appear in seminars and on television shows. Some of them have their own how-to TV programs.

Tournament fishermen use spinning, spincasting or baitcasting gear. Flyfishing hasn't worked out and fly rods in a boat with a plugger or spinfisherman have been judged too inconvenient.

Most of the big tournaments do not accommodate women competitors and it was inevitable that the ladies should have their own organization and their own tourneys. Their association, of course, retained the bass fishing tone. They are not Bass-Fishing Women or Bassing Ladies. They are "Bassin' Gals" so they have maintained tradition, even though their jumpsuits may fit differently.

In Europe it is completely different. Those who have seen millions of dollars in gleaming sportsfishermen booming out to sea at the start of a tuna tournament or have heard the two-cycle song of speeding bass boats echoing in the canyons of an Arkansas impoundment would take a second look at Europe's "matchmen."

Match fishing is done from land and the quarry is rough fish. The fishermen work from numbered stakes set in a row on the bank and are not allowed to infringe upon other "swims." It started in the last century, begun by working-class fishermen unable to reach trout and salmon waters—or unable to gain access to them. Some of the big matches draw as many as 5000 or more contestants, generally appearing as teams from local clubs. In addition to sizable cash prizes, bookmakers add their attraction.

In some of the biggest events any form of live or dead fish or any kind of artificial lure is prohibited. The matchmen use hand catapults for throwing "ground bait" or chum to attract fish to their swims and away from their neighbors'. The rods run from 30-foot "roach poles" to tiny wands for catching the shoreline tiddlers. A match can be won with a swarm of tiny fish, all of which must be kept in a storage net for release once they have been weighed. The best of such fishermen become well known both in England and on the mainland. It is competition, as far from the American bass tournament as the bass tournament is from the tuna match.

The tackle for such fishing is worked to a fine art, the rods using sensitive "swing tips" and "quiver tips" to indicate a nibble and what direction a fish is taking. Hooks, of course, are in all sizes, some

Like maneuvering landing craft, these bass tournament boats
come in to have their catches checked by officials.

smaller than most trout fishermen ever see, and a top professional might have literally hundreds of bobbers to suit various situations.

Like it or not, competition is a permanent part of sport angling. It can be a nuisance, but modern tackle has been developed by it and competitive organizations have been the backbone of the fisherman's fight to protect his sport.

CHAPTER TWELVE

WITH AUTHORITY

Famous fishermen tend to be teachers, writers or inventors, and often all three. In picking out the leaders I've tried to accent concrete contributions to the sport, which leaves out some of the best angling authors and puts in some whose prose doesn't exactly sparkle. In fact, some of the most informative fishing material I've read has been presented with all the artistic charm of a legal notice.

Trout fishermen generally write prettiest, some of them managing to decorate a belabored subject until you forget you aren't reading anything new. Izaak Walton was a whiz at that. But since trout fishermen tend to willingly absorb literary punishment, they turn some stuff that would be too dull to see print in any other field into good sellers.

Saltwater authors make things adventurous, and since their sport is on a larger scale and occasionally even a bit dangerous, that's probably justified. Ernest Hemingway wrote of billfishing the way he wrote of war, strafed sharks with submachine guns and endowed big fish with fearsome personalities. Kip Farrington, one of the most successful 20th century big-fish catchers, equated his achievement with big-time athletics.

The bass fishermen of recent years scorn any sort of arty approach to their literature and often manage to make their instructional theses read like antiseptic graffiti. They're a little short on pretty sunsets and songbirds. And by gosh, they're a little short on humor too. Ed Zern is a trout fisherman.

Leaving the early British authorities to their respective centuries, we find Americans beginning to take pen in hand in the 19th. As far as I can tell, Thad Norris came the closest of any American to Walton's approach, devoting some type to the beauties of the countryside and getting philosophical over angling as a whole. He didn't get his *American Angler's Book* on the shelves until 1864. His work had color and told of fishing method.

Most historians list Jerome Smith's *Natural History of the Fishes of Massachusetts, Embracing a Practical Essay on Angling* as the first American treatise and it showed up in 1833. For those who feel real sport angling didn't get going until we had split-bamboo trout rods, dry flies and striper clubs, Smith isn't too informational but you can always use art critic language and call his work "primitive."

George Washington Bethune, a minister, edited the first American edition of Walton's *The Compleat Angler* in 1847, doing it a bit sneakily because of the tenuous status of fishermen with regard to religion, and with disapproval of dissolute Charles Cotton. Bethune deserves mention because he did some good writing in his commentary. Like other authors before 1900, Bethune filled considerable space selling fishing to his readers. Maybe they overdid it because I suspect most of their clients were already hooked.

Thad Norris is fun to read, especially in some of his comments on fly fishing—opinions that had been common before him and which were repeated constantly for the next hundred years. He said:

"An extensive knowledge of flies and their names can hardly be of much practical advantage. Many a rustic adept is ignorant of a book ever having been written on fly-fishing, and knows the few flies he uses only by his own limited vocabulary. One of the most accomplished fly-fishers I ever met with has told me that his first essay was with the scalp of a red-headed woodpecker tied to the top of his hook."

Flies and trout had been the theme of a great majority of fishing literature up until the black bass how-to books of the 1970s. For a time the trout was so dominant that trout methods came first, even if you were choking them with worms.

To be a famous author or authority you have to get it between hard covers. Some of the best outdoor writing and some of the most valuable information has come from the pages of magazines and newspapers, partly because the authors are more relaxed, especially the columnists, who don't have to make sales by hyperbole or shock. Some of the best has turned brittle and yellow in library files and some of the names are forgotten because they never appeared on books.

Spirit of the Times started in 1831 and for the next 30 years or so ran frequent articles on the outdoors, especially fishing, although it was not purely an outdoor publication. It was strong on horse racing. Henry William Herbert (Frank Forester) was a frequent contributor and rates special notice because he covered the field, whether or not his work was literary.

Herbert's personal history is spicy. He came to the United States in 1831 from England when he was only 24 years old, a member of the nobility and evidently fleeing some sort of scandal that was never unearthed by American researchers. He lived largely on a trust established by his father and when he began to write for *Spirit of the Times* he took the pen name Frank Forester, probably because such a pursuit wasn't considered quite respectable. He wrote a how-to book called *Fishing With Hook and Line* and also *Frank Forester's Fishing of the United States and British Provinces.*

Forester gave sound fishing instruction and he began to make saltwater sport fishing respectable. Even then, he said fly fishing for striped bass was coastal sport surpassed only by salmon fishing. He advocated fly fishing for herring and said good things about fly fishing for shad, explaining that satisfactory shad flies could be had at Conroy's on Fulton Street in New York. These pronouncements have been swept under the rug by some historians who would like to have them discovered much later. I am sure, however, that the originator of the 20th century Harold Gibbs Striper Fly or the first makers of the shiny little shad streamers will concede him room in history. Forester somewhat befogs the discovery of the trolling spoon by Julio Buel by casually mentioning the common pewter spoon as a tool of eastern bluefishermen, but what difference does it make? Buel put the thing on the market.

Anyway, Herbert was party to an unhappily brief marriage in 1858 and ended the Frank Forester story by shooting himself shortly afterward. Perhaps he was the first American "outdoor writer"; the others of his time tended to do their fishing material incidentally.

Louis Agassiz, Swiss naturalist and teacher, came to America in 1845 after his career was well under way and he was already highly regarded as a European naturalist-scientist. Apparently he was the first biologist to make an organized study of the world's fishes, and although he was not personally responsible for any advancement of sport angling as such, his studies were a boon to those who worked at it. During his lifetime were some of the first purely scientific expeditions for study of saltwater biology; as a teacher he made more than a start in a difficult field. A little out of character for a dedicated student was his reputation as a champion fencer. In his youth, he was willing to demonstrate this skill to any and all with little provocation.

Among the very earliest American fishing writers, John J. Brown, a New York tackle dealer, wrote *The American Angler's Guide* in 1845. That one is pretty scarce and collectors pay well for it. Brown had some things to say about fly fishing and most of the grubbers of American fishing history have sought the fly information above all.

Throughout early American sport fishing runs the name of Seth Green (1817-1888), the "father of fish culture." He wrote some instructional material on fish propagation and authored *Home Fishing and Home Water*, but he is less known than some who caught fewer fish and certainly did less for the sport.

Cliff Netherton says Green was the "first outstanding casting champion." In 1862 Green was awarded first prize "for the best general excellence in the use of the rod" and his distance fly casting won a number of tournaments. Even then, he was reaching nearly 100 feet.

Green very nearly covered the field, having been a commercial fisherman in his youth. Stories of stand fishing for stripers of the North Atlantic coast mention Green, even at an advanced age, staying put while his stand took solid green water. He built the Caledonia Fish Hatchery in 1864 and was superintendent of it, also serving as a New York State Fish Commissioner. He took Atlantic shad to California for the Sacramento River in 1871, quite an achievement with the primitive fish transportation available at the time. That shad planting was highly successful as Pacific Coasters took the shad to their bosom and have worked it over with light tackle and enthusiasm ever since.

Green is credited with bringing the rainbow trout eastward, a move that had a great deal more effect than any relocation of shad; but then, the rainbow was going to make it anyway and I suspect a great many busybodies were involved in its migration, officially and unofficially. The rainbow saved many of the eastern trout streams, even over the outraged cries of those who wanted the native brookie or nothing. Anyway, Green made big contributions in several ways.

I Go A-Fishing was written in 1873 by W. C. Prime and contained a great deal on trout fishing. Prime, who may not have been quoted as much as some of the other writers of his time, wrote several things in the outdoor field, though some were not exactly nuts-and-bolts fishing.

More than 100 years later there was a movement against fishing for sport, led by those who felt it was improper to gain pleasure from a fish's discomfort. Most sport anglers felt such an idea was alarmingly new. Let us go back and look at something Prime wrote. One of his characters says:

"In the name of sense, man, if God made fish to be eaten, what difference does it make if I enjoy the killing of them before I eat them? You would have none but a fisherman by trade do it, and then you would have him utter a sigh, a prayer, and a pious ejaculation at each cod or haddock that he killed; and if by chance the old fellow sitting in the boat at his work, should for a moment think there was, after all, a little fun and a little pleasure in his business, you would have him take a round turn with his line, and drop on his knees to ask forgiveness for the sin of thinking there was sport in fishing."

The language was slightly modernized but the same thing was written dozens of times in the 1970s when Jacques Costeau, famous naturalist and super-showman, said that fishing for sport is a perversion. Sport fishermen got up in arms and outdoor writers irately lashed out with their typewriters.

Robert Barnwell Roosevelt, an uncle of Theodore, was writing his books in the 1860s, and since he was addicted to rather flowery prose, even for that day, it's fun to make a little fun of him. Arnold Gingrich dug up this quote on trout fishing from R. B. R., which appeared as quoted by Thad Norris:

"How pleasant is the sport to deftly throw the long line and small fly, with the pliant single-handed rod, and with eye and nerve on the strain, to watch the loveliest darling of the wave, the spotted niad, dart from her mossy bed, leap high into the air, carrying the strange deception in her mouth, and turning in her flight, plunge back to her crystal home."

Norris thought that was overly flashy stuff back in his day and it's considerably richer than the current most flowery trout material. I don't think Bill Dance could use it on his TV fishing show and it will never be inscribed on anybody's bass boat.

Roosevelt complimented Seth Green by saying, "He most shines when he is wielding the light but powerful fly rod that he loves and understands so well. He gazes far off over the rippled water looking after the falling fly, as time after time he lifts the long line with a powerful yet elegant motion and swinging it far behind him, casts it forward with the perfection of easy force."

Roosevelt was a lawyer and perhaps such flights were a relief from the perusal of less colorful torts and contracts. A catalog of *Anglers & Shooters Bookshelf* mentions that a copy of Roosevelt's *Superior Fishing* ($42.50) contains the first mention of waterproof silk lines.

We have Theodore Gordon in another chapter on fly fishing but said little of his work as a writer. Gordon certainly isn't the only well-to-do recluse who has devoted his life to fishing, but he was a sort of link between the old and the new since he extended his own experiments by making contact with Britain's Frederic Halford, getting some of his dry flies and going on from there. Perhaps Gordon got one little jump on the British because he had to contend with faster water and needed flies that rode high. For that matter, American fishermen still lead in buoyant drys that will bounce over a waterfall.

Gordon's image has been burnished by John McDonald, a New York writer (and an editor of *Fortune*) who dug into the matter with other enthusiasts and located Gordon's grave. Gordon, born in 1854, died in 1915 and has a hallowed stature among American fly fishermen. McDonald manages to make him a sort of immortal shade along the Neversink and other Eastern streams.

Gordon wrote well himself and contributed to the British *Fishing Gazette,* something not common for provincials. He wrote in 1906:

"I see that a writer in the *New York Sun* states that dryfly fishing is unknown in this country, or, if known to a few, is not practiced successfully. He is quite mistaken. The dry fly has been used on many streams in the Middle States for years. It was not unknown to Uncle Thaddeus Norris, who wrote the *American Angler's Book* about 1863. He gives an instance of great success with dry fly on the Willowemock, when wet fly was useless."

That doesn't mean, of course, that Norris' dry flies were necessarily tied, doped or fished in modern style. Gordon has received much more credit for dry flies than did Uncle Thad.

Mary Orvis Marbury of the fly-tying and rod-making Orvises produced *Favorite Flies and their Histories* in 1892. Austin Hogan, the angling historian, calls it "a colorful, romantic and charming Victorian presentation."

Almost a century later, Colonel Joseph D. Bates, Jr., researched other kinds of flies and came forth with some impressive volumes. His *Streamers & Bucktails, the Big Fish Flies* (1979) is especially attractive because Bates is one of those characters who brings forth long letters from those who fish and study fishing.

We've said a great deal about Dr. James A. Henshall in other places so I won't go much further into his story, but like Gordon, he is a link to the past, having lived, fished and written during the transition from bass poles to casting rods. He wrote about bass in a world of trout lovers. My somewhat weathered copy of *Book of the Black Bass* came from Pete Siman, book collector and famous fisherman, best known for his Florida Keys records. There is a thrill in opening any old fishing book but an inscription on the flyleaf of this one stops me cold. In a beautiful hand (people learned penmanship in those days) it says: "To Eddie from Lena, Christmas 1909." Lena chose a nice gift and I wonder who she and Eddie were.

Edward Ringwood Hewitt (1866-1951) concentrated on trout and salmon, and if you could have only one book on salmonid fishing his *A Trout and Salmon Fisherman for Seventy-five Years,* compiled when he was past 80 years old, is about as good a choice as any, even now. In that book Hewitt used much of the material in his earlier texts including *Secrets of the Salmon, Telling On the Trout, Handbook of Fly Fishing* and *Nymph Fly Fishing.*

Hewitt was born to wealth and spent most of his life angling and researching angling subjects. He was a practical fisherman who won casting tournaments late in the last century and as a member of the Angler's Club of New York he participated in English meets as well as domestic ones. His contributions include the "skater" flies, those dry, spidery creations that are rediscovered regularly. He also led in dryfly fishing for Atlantic salmon, a practice at one time considered unfeasible if not impossible. Most impressive is his detailed study of how trout live and feed, revealing details that appear again and again in later books.

Hewitt was a fish culturist, a tournament caster, a photographer, an engineer, an inventor and a writer. He designed bamboo rods and had them made up by the Leonard Rod Company—and built a few himself. I don't know just when the trout's surface window of vision was first understood, but Hewitt's explanation of how the fisherman and his flies are seen by the quarry is about as good as anything that has appeared since then. It was illustrated with photographs that took considerable ingenuity to obtain, especially with the technical limitations of his day.

Fishing schools were attracting big enrollments in the 1970s.
This one is practicing at the Orvis plant in Vermont.

Hewitt quotes are pretty meaty. Get this:

> "The ancients wrote of the three ages of man; I propose to write of the three ages of the fisherman.
> "When he wants to catch all the fish he can.
> "When he strives to catch the largest fish.
> "When he studies to catch the most difficult fish he can find, requiring the greatest skill and most refined tackle, caring more for the sport than the fish."

In his later years he told interviewers that he had caught a lot of fish in his lifetime and that he was now less concerned with catching fish than in having fish to catch. It may be that Hewitt let a little personal ego creep in now and then but he had a right if anyone had. He was a brilliant, busy man who did his thing through built-in drive when he could have loafed a long lifetime.

With Hewitt ends the easy part. After Hewitt we have authorities who have been known to fishermen still living, some of them having come on in a fishing boom that has lasted from 1945 into the 80s. Some of the very best of the writers and teachers have contributed no tactics or tackle of their own but have covered the field charmingly, and have no ambition to be known as inventors or discoverers.

Alfred W. Miller (Sparse Grey Hackle) is a fishing student and humorist who has written introductions and commentaries to endless works on fishing (especially trout angling). He has been around for many years and can deliver first-hand information on things that readers think of as being from a misty time learned about only through hearsay. Miller is a good writer whose own work ranges from clever humor to history.

Roderick Haig-Brown came to Canada from England and his books can be regarded as classics. The best known titles are *Fisherman's Spring, Fisherman's Winter, Fisherman's Summer* and *Fisherman's Fall,* mostly applied to the rivers of the Canadian Pacific Coast. This is moody material and informational as it relates the natural history of game fishes.

Haig-Brown was a skilled fisherman but made no point of his abilities in that category (when someone wanted to make motion pictures of him fishing he said he didn't think he could cast well enough for that). He wrote *Return to the River*, published in 1941, as the life history of a Pacific salmon, and his other titles appeared up into the 60s. Although his background was English he avoided the British traditions in most of his work, something that endeared him to fishermen who had never stayed awake over the question of whether a wet fly downstream was ethical. He brought more understanding of environmental problems, especially of anadromous fish, and did it in a way that made it stick.

Ray Bergman was one of the best-known angling columnists and book authors, putting plain fishing facts into language that has informed two generations. His book *Trout* arrived in 1938 and is still quoted by trout fishermen. His book on bass, of course, didn't get so much attention although it was just as good, and is seldom quoted by bass fishermen, who don't read so much and are likely to prefer something from the new school of depthfinders and electric motors.

Van Campen Heilner, born in 1899, wrote a great deal of saltwater material, adventure as well as how-to, and he was one of the editors of *Field & Stream*. His work on saltwater, especially inshore and surf fishing, came before the rush to the beaches and his *Salt Water Fishing*, a big seller, was dated 1937. He was a great traveler so his work gives a broad coverage of the subject.

Not long ago I found myself accidentally aboard a yachtish cruiser formerly owned by Heilner. The current owner was a little vague about its background but it was fun to run down its history through new engines and occasional refitting. Although it had been a long time since Heilner and his friends had lived aboard it there was no doubt that it had been built on purpose. I suppose it's still operating.

He didn't really write his copy in acid, but Jason Lucas, long-time fishing editor of *Sports Afield*, had an opinion on almost everything related to angling. During his tenure he was the best known of all the fishing scribes. His special wrath was saved for incompetent clerks. His favorite name for them was *panty salesmen*, which he felt indicated the peak of angling incompetence. His arbitrary opinions about fly rods were unshakeable and often repeated, and except that he scorned any stick which didn't exactly fit his formula, they were logical enough.

Lucas fished alone most of the time and for years used a little Penn Yan cartop boat with an Evinrude motor. Since his fishing authorship required frequent photographs, he had a camera mounted in the bow of the little rig, facing the stern and focused on him—so when Lucas needed a photo of Lucas in action all he had to do was press a foot switch. He also had one of the larger and better-filled tackle boxes in the business. It may not be germaine to his fishing qualifications, but he smoked a pipe with such diligence that he often laid it beside his plate as he ate and took a few pulls between courses.

He worked the trout streams, mainly alone, and he spent many of his winters in Florida pursuing tarpon and snook, but his most dramatic expertise concerned black bass. He was one of the first fishermen to move off the shoreline to seek bass at greater depths and over the "structure" that was to be well known a few years later. That was how he gained his earliest fishing reputation. He preserved his image with opinionated writing, especially in the crisp answers he served to reader's inquiries at *Sports Afield*.

When a reader asked if he knew a way to prevent a fish from jumping and thus throwing a hook, Lucas answered that he knew how to do that but wouldn't tell. It was unsportsmanlike, he said.

He had a fault, a reluctance to consider matters outside his own fishing experience. His heyday immediately preceded the scientific bass fishing that came in the 60s, when Buck Perry preached gouging the bottom.

Al McClane, author of numerous books and world-traveling fisherman, held forth as angling editor of *Field & Stream* through many of the post-World War II years. His *McClane's Standard Fishing Encyclopedia* is probably the most comprehensive fishing volume ever produced and grows fatter with succeeding editions. Later, he was noted as an authority on where-to-go, but during his early days with *Field & Stream* he was especially strong on ultra-light "threadline" spinning for trout, a field that really met with public interest. McClane is respected as a superior fly fisherman and he has written of wide experiences with flies in Europe, South America and the Caribbean.

McClane's background is scientific and he can switch into highly technical discourses when he feels like it, whether the subject be entomology or the physics of rod construction. You can almost sense him saying, "Now I'll give them something technical," but he can be an entertaining storyteller too. Related to and also outside of his fishing, he is a gourmet cook and author.

Ted Trueblood came on as an "all-around" outdoor author and has had a penchant for writing how-to material with just enough catchy phrases to be remembered as an individual. Some years back he was involved in a friendly feud with Ed Zern, the outdoor humorist. Both of them worked for *Field & Stream* and Zern raised the question that maybe there really was no such person as Ted Trueblood, implying that Trueblood's name might be a phony, rigged to sound like an all-American sportsman. Some readers accepted the tongue-in-cheek attack for the real thing and magazine sales boomed. Trueblood staunchly defended his existence. Finally, there was a photo of him and Zern together, and after that it was popularly believed that Trueblood was real.

In addition to his pleasant and informing columns, books and articles, Trueblood made some concrete additions to angling. When the tournament casters came forth with their fly rod shooting heads and monofilament running line, such gear was seized happily by double-hauling steelheaders, Trueblood included. But Trueblood went another notch and arranged a fly-fishing system in which he used shooting heads for everything, including dry-fly fishing for trout. He said you could carry all sorts of heads in your vest and fasten them to your running line for any condition. The system was not widely accepted by trout anglers, except for streamer fishing, but the shooting head certainly got a boost from Trueblood. He helped popularize "impression" nymphs with vague, fuzzy outlines.

He wrote some highly informational things on baitcasting for large trout, explaining a system for spoon manipulation on the steep shorelines of lakes. He told how to get the most of the spoon in fast water as spinning was becoming popular. Spinning reels began to take over from such as the Pfluger Supreme turning spool, but the methods are still the same.

In salt water, award-winning Frank Woolner has been the chronicler of the high surf; he and Hal Lyman at *Salt Water Sportsman* magazine have probably done more to promote saltwater angling, especially inshore, than anyone else. Lyman may be slightly less known than Woolner as a how-to and mood author but his international stature in saltwater gamefish management is greater than the casual reader may realize. Lyman's seagoing background includes skippering a U.S. Navy destroyer in the Pacific, so he probably is not inclined toward seasickness, and Woolner, a World War II tanker, has withstood some jouncing himself.

Frank Moss, one-time charter boatman, comes very close to being a final authority on offshore operations and has written columns, books and articles on that subject for a lot of years. It is hard to avoid thinking of him and Jim Martenhoff when saltwater navigation is the subject. There have been many other top commentators on boats and fishing separately, but these veterans have spliced the two together in pleasant harmony, despite Martenhoff's tours into the galley as a seafood gourmet to rival Al McClane.

Joe Brooks was a flyfishing celebrity for more than 20 years, a less-recognized expert for much longer than that, being traditional as to tackle and method but accepting new things after they had been around for a time. He bugged for bass with mighty bamboo rods that weighed 8 ounces, and he made fly fishing for bonefish. He fished worldwide but was especially known for his activities in Argentina, the Florida Keys and Montana, where his grave overlooks the Yellowstone River. Except for the West Coasters he was the leading proponent of the big rod and the long fly line, before 100-pound fly rod tarpon became commonplace. He accepted sinking lines and shock tippets rather grudgingly but was still around when they came into their own.

When scientific bass fishing came in the late 60s, there were literally dozens of new television shows and countless books and magazines on the subject. A complete list of instructors is impossible, but it is safe to put Roland Martin at the head of the list, a personable young fellow who became the biggest tourney winner of all, looked handsome on his television shows and filled halls with his seminars. Bill Dance comes to mind as another top technician of the depthfinder and bass boat, also a pleasing television personality who wasn't above appearing with a small aluminum boat and other simple gear when conditions required it.

Of the how-to television performers, Gadabout Gaddis was one of a kind, flying his own airplane to the good fishing spots and relating his activities in a first person play-by-play. Gaddis had been a roving fisherman and tackle salesman long before World War II, but it was his television show that captured public interest later on. When he went into semi-retirement in the 1970s, many a promoter scrounged for a similar character with a similar approach. All of the instructor-showmen have used a little of the Gaddis format but there has been only one Gadabout. He was at his best in explaining bluegill fishing while competitors of the tube wrestled marlin or giant tuna.

As a how-to man it is hard to beat Mark Sosin, a businesslike writer who specializes in inshore salt water but has done a little of everything. I am not touting Sosin as the originator of any school of fishing but as a student of the whole works. He has written some fine books with technical experts in various fishing fields. This doesn't mean Sosin is not a fine fisherman himself but he is quite willing to collaborate with a specialist, so put him down as one of the top teachers.

That brings us to Bernard (Lefty) Kreh. Like some other performers, Kreh was famous on the way to his skills and was successfully teaching fly casting to others when he was just another good fly fisherman. But before someone could come forward to make him look bad he had learned the game so well that *nobody* could make him look bad. He had a thousand little gimmicks to get your attention but his basic virtue is solid flycasting method, and although he has not been a tournament performer, I suspect he could have made it there. He's been a columnist for newspapers and magazines for a long time and says Joe Brooks and Tom McNally *(Chicago Tribune)* gave him much of his start.

Parodoxically, Kreh is a humorist who is an after-dinner winner with fine story telling, but his writing, while good-natured, doesn't often get into straight comedy.

Stuart Apte, who has taken his fishing very, very seriously, made his reputation in the Florida Keys. As a youth he fished there in non-stop marathons, during which he confesses he lost considerable sleep and even a little weight. Then, after flying navy warplanes, he became a Pan American flier, only to quit to guide on the Keys flats.

No one doubts that Apte found the fish and knew how to hook them, but his life-and-death approach caused him to occasionally address his clients in terminology which football coaches reserve for athletes who forget the playbook. He was a perfectionist in a field where few are perfect.

Apte went back to Pan American and continued to get into the record books through his achievements with light tackle. He made some fine motion pictures of inshore saltwater fishing, wrote articles for outdoor magazines, fished around the world and remained an authority on some of the fine points, including knots and lures. People like Vic Dunaway of Florida and Pete Perinchief of Bermuda are equally expert in the very little things (while being expert anglers), although they have not assaulted the record books with such enthusiasm.

Lee Wulff's reputation as an outdoorsman goes back to his Alaskan origin and his operation of a salmon camp in Newfoundland. He really worked over the Atlantic salmon with the aid of his float plane. A Newfie guide passed judgment with the simple statement, "There was a man!"

Wulff continued to make significant contributions into his seventies. While he wrote authoritative works on Atlantic salmon, flies and offshore angling, he and his wife Joan Salvato, a former casting champion, conducted a fishing school. Wulff, who has some flies named after him, had a flair for the extraordinary and caught big Atlantic salmon with tiny flies and tiny bamboo rods at a time when big two-handers were popular. He put offshore fly fishermen in their place by going after marlin with what he called "standard" fly tackle, scorning the big reels with the heavy-duty drags. It's said that he invented the fishing vest, but that may have come in rather gradually. He certainly invented a salmon tailer.

Anyone who delves into Ernest Schwiebert's enormous two-volume work, *Trout,* might decide after a few hundred pages that this is more than he really wanted to know about the subject, but Schwiebert has long been an idol of scientific trout fishermen. He's traveled the world for a variety of trouts in addition to more than his share of Atlantic salmon.

It is in the nymph business that Schwiebert takes his bows as a master, being a wizard at the rather occult matter of hooking large trout which have eaten an artificial nymph bouncing along the bottom on a long leader. His entomology is what first made him famous among trout anglers and he really dug into the identification of insects. He's also one of the most knowing in the field of trout rise forms and has found names for them. When his text on nymphs was successful, he commented: "Who'd have thought there were that many nuts?"

With and after Schwiebert have come a parade of fly fishermen for trout who have taken some little phase of the business, introduced some new flies, used their original ideas as a reader trap, and then done a good job of presenting general knowledge on trout and trout catching. The "catch" subject can be special nymphs, moving dry flies, streamers, wet flies or whatever. I have no intention of discrediting them as experts although it is in the general field that their work is likely to be most valuable.

One special area, covered by Vince Marinaro in *A Modern Dry Fly Code,* deals largely with Pennsylvania's Letort and other similar streams that are short on mayfly hatches and require unconventional gadgetry. Charles K. Fox, also a Letort operator, bolstered an already considerable angling reputation with *This Wonderful World of Trout,* one of the better texts.

Paul R. Needham presented *Trout Streams* in 1938 and went into the elemental biology of the subject, a part that has been widely ignored by anglers who frequently wonder where the fish have gone from their favorite waters. The book has since been republished and is a basic text for everybody who fishes trout.

Charles Ritz, a famous caster and representative of the hotel chain family, was for many years a student of the miniscule factors involved in putting a fly from here to there. I can't say that he invented any specific moves, but he watched the winners of the casting platform and put emphasis on the phases that mattered.

I can't say that Bill Schadt of the Pacific coast has done all that much teaching but he has been spied on by many of the best, such as his artist friend Russ Chatham, who throws heavy lines in the same league and can be induced to write about it at intervals. These people are regarded by tournament casters as transplants of competitive casting from such as the Golden Gate Casting Club to the steelhead and salmon rivers. Chatham is likely to tape the guides on a rod blank to avoid the bother of thread and, like Schadt, fishes for salmon at depths that fly fishermen are supposed to ignore. When someone told him that leadcore lines weren't sporting, he responded that he couldn't see what harm it did as long as he put the fish back anyway. There is only one of each of these characters.

John Alden Knight put together the solunar tables which shook the entire fishing world and keep shaking it. The major and minor feeding periods have caused considerable fussing through the years and continue to be valued by sportsmen. There is no argument that there are certain times when wildlife (and domestic life too) is on the move, and Knight, an angling writer, coupled the "moon up, moon down" business to fishing.

Most anglers immediately came forth with the idea that the time to go fishing is when you can get away, but there were thousands who tested Knight's theory. The consensus was that although many other factors might be more potent than the location of the moon with relation to the earth the tables were helpful, and "other things being equal," they indicated better fishing. Anyway, as Knight reported long after his system was being published in thousands of publications, the solunar tables were helpful enough to make a living for a couple of families for a good many years, and they're still popular. Few fishing columnists have not received a query as to "whether there's anything to it."

We'll stick Grits Gresham in here, even though he's primarily a hunter in the minds of readers of his shooting column in *Sports Afield*. Gresham, much better known now than he was then, wrote the first of the black bass books that covered the new school of bass fishing, which involved many of the modern gadgets and certainly stressed the "structure" fishing mentioned glibly by millions of later fishermen. He didn't delve as deeply into water or technique as some who came after him but he produced a good start.

Books on both Pacific and Atlantic salmon by Anthony Netboy, appearing in the early 70s, have become invaluable to a generation that is trying to bring back the "king of gamefish," especially on the New England coast. Netboy did a research job.

We leave out hundreds of the greatest, especially guides who may have been responsible for the theories of famous writers—theories that have sometimes been pirated, but generally have simply been credited to a writer rather than to the original proponent, whom he may have quoted. We have tried to stress those who have had an influence on the sport, and had to skip thousands of the world's best anglers, unknown masters who couldn't care less. They make their livings at something else.

CHAPTER THIRTEEN

BIG CHANGES

Everything changed after World War II. The main factors were spinning reels, glass rods, nylon, the Tennessee Valley Authority and new fishermen.

Spinning gear caused the biggest convulsion. Here was a casting method that anyone could learn in a few minutes. The pupil might not know where his lure was headed but he could make it go. Most new fishermen thought spinning was a sudden breakthrough, but the fact is it had been around in one form or another for 60 years. Peter Malloch of Scotland made an early reel that cast from a stationary spool (as in the modern versions) but the spool was swung to the side and revolved during the retrieve.

That design had some line twisting disadvantages but they could be minimized in heavy-duty equipment through the use of good swivels. The same system was employed into the 1980s, especially in Australia, with the Alvey. The big spool made for a simple tool that could stand abuse.

Most spinning reels were used with monofilament lines which were a little stiff and wiry at first, but improved rapidly. There was a

*Reel repairmen sometimes despaired of fixing some of
the first spinning reels, hurriedly built after
World War II.*

great deal of trouble with bails and they still cause most spinning reel problems. Manual reels were quickly popular with some serious fishermen who figured it was as easy to educate a forefinger as it had been to educate a thumb for plugging reels, but manuals remain in the minority, despite their durable simplicity.

At first the spinning outfit was cursed for its inaccuracy, but when casters learned to feather the line as it came off the open spool they came very near to what baitcasters could do. It was difficult to design the pushbutton reel so that a cast could be slowed gradually but that came eventually and accuracy improved. However, the closed-face reel is basically a shorter-ranged tool.

The spinning thing got silly in the early 50s when some of its opponents announced that it meant the death of all other forms of casting and that it might be necessary to pass new laws to keep it from completely wiping out fish populations. But it accomplished two things: it made it possible to cast lures much smaller and lighter than conventional reels would throw and it opened the way for millions of new fishermen. With tiny lures it bridged the gap between the fly rod and the plugging rig, and many fish loved the little baits.

The Illingworth reel, patented much earlier in England, worked on the same principle as later models. The Luxor reel came to the United States in the 30s, marketed by Bache Brown for Pezon-Michel of France, but the war stopped that. When spinning really got going in the late 40s, it came with a few high-grade reels and some appalling junk.

The junk came because builders and importers saw that a great many new fishermen were going to get spinning gear and that the market was going to depend on price. Many were what tackle dealers called "throw away" outfits, intended to last for one fishing trip, and sometimes they didn't even do that. One importer exhibited a boxful of Japanese imports, all different. He said they cost him roughly a dollar apiece in this country and he wondered which would be the best one for his line.

There were precision reels too, mostly European imports. Probably the most popular one through the years has been the Mitchell, which at first had its ups and downs in quality but holds a big market.

The closed-face or pushbutton models became known as spincasting reels. They were the simplest to operate, and the makers had to make them at low prices because they were the favorites of less sophisticated fishermen. Some pushbuttons were pretty flimsy. If they could have sold for $100 instead of $10 they would have gotten off to a better start. Later, some well made pushbuttons suffered for the sins of the junkers.

For a number of years there was a relative slump in sales of turning spool casting reels, and some fly fishermen were converted to the new method. Even in the 50s, many baitcasting reels still had "flywheel action" that demanded heavy baits although light alloy spools had been available for 50 years.

Nylon gears were used to make the casting reels faster. It was freespooling that really brought the casting reel back, and although it was nothing new, very few fishermen used it until the Swedish Ambassadeur broke the ice in that direction.

Finally, spinning found its niche as another very good way to fish, and while it became the most popular of all, plugcasting and fly fishing remained. Eventually, most spinfishing organizations concluded that the way line was spooled didn't make all that much difference, and in most cases spinning records were combined with those of turning spools. There were still some "throw-away" spincast outfits but there was some fine precision equipment too.

For the most part, even the modern freespool casting reels are confined to the heavier lures and only a die-hard lover of baitcasting will use anything less than ¼ ounce. This leaves little jigs and small spinner-fly combinations to the spinfisherman. Before spinning came along fly fishermen strained everything by throwing plugs, spoons and spinner-fly lures, a job the fly rod has been mercifully exempted from. The spinning rod proved superior in throwing soft natural baits.

Monofilament gave strength with small diameter and tough resistance to abrasion, and cast beautifully on both spinning and conventional reels once the wire was taken out of it. It is relatively inexpensive to manufacture. Along with it came braided nylon that didn't rot easily, and most of the troubles of silk and linen disappeared.

Fiberglass rods came in the 40s and at first the best known was the Howald process type, developed by Dr. Arthur Howald, using a balsa wood mandrel that stayed inside the shaft. Shakespeare took the lead and for years the white rod with its spiral markings was far out ahead.

*First of the popular modern freespooling casting reels
was the Swedish Ambassadeur.
(Photo by Joel Arrington)*

Those weren't the first glass rods, though; Dr. Glen Havens of National City, California, who had been experimenting with fiberglass and resins since the mid-30s, is credited with the first one.

After the Shakespeare came a flood of glass and by the 50s many firms built complete rods or rod blanks. Several endeavored to make a special color stand for quality. Some colored the blanks to resemble wood. The glossy black Harnells were especially successful as surf sticks and tournament distance fly rods, although they served elsewhere as well.

Some glass rod builders found that superior fishing action does not necessarily indicate durability, and when some of the most reliable companies guaranteed their rods against breakage they found themselves in trouble. For example, the early guaranteed Harnell baitcasting rods beloved by some top casters tended to break in two with a snap cast. Breakage was the number one problem in those days; some of the tackle firms found their carefully made rods would literally shatter with severe treatment or fatigue. But designs quickly improved, and by about 1955 it was possible to build in almost any action desired and match the individuals of a given model.

Solid glass rods were inexpensive to build and incredibly tough, but they were rather heavy and except for very cheap models were relegated to extremely heavy duty in trolling and boat fishing with large baits. In glass, as with other materials, there was a period of advertising that stressed designs that could be tied in knots—a quality not of much use in fishing.

Although glass quickly backed most steel rods off the market, it could not displace bamboo in light fly rods. By 1965 there weren't many bass buggers and saltwater fishermen who preferred bamboo, and about that time the fly fishermen began to announce that although they never would give up their light cane trout rods, they insisted on glass for anything that took more than a No. 8 line.

Number designation for fly tackle came slowly, finally accepted by the American Fishing Tackle Manufacturers' Association to replace the old letter system for line and rod size. It brought much-needed standardization. Before it became popular the world was full of fly rods that wouldn't work because their inexperienced owners had bought lines that didn't fit them. A clerk who had walked over from the gun department wasn't much help.

Glass or the later graphite could never carry the prestige of split bamboo, but some craftsmen have been able to do wonderful things by judicious reinforcement of glass sections. Whether fine glass can really match bamboo in light sticks is debatable but really costly glass scares off buyers. Since there are mass-produced glass blanks that match each other beautifully and are inexpensive, fishermen are slow to accept the costs of custom glass.

Graphite costs more than glass but it has remarkable qualities for casting tools. First embraced by fly fishermen, it is used in baitcasting and spinning rods too, although the latter are less demanding as to casting action. Graphite went through the same stages as glass had: the period of breakage that kept worried builders poring over their books, the comparison to earlier materials. Obviously, it had to be guaranteed against breakage or it could never make the grade. It

Big government surplus rubber liferafts were popular for river floating after World War II. Boats were greatly refined later. This one was fresh from military surplus in the 1950s.

became a super material but the little bamboo trout rods are still preferred by some connoisseurs. Popular by 1975, graphite had been in use since utilized by William Watt of England in 1965.

Next came boron and finally it began to appear that there was no crime in mixing space-age materials for optimum results. Now, although some superior rods use them, the combinations are a little vague and catchy trade names confuse buyers. The main thing is that most of the rods are good. Like lure making, rod building is a shadowy area dependent upon the fickle allegiance of anglers, who have driven many a well-meaning firm into bankruptcy. No one can say a rod casts well or badly except as it performs for him, and much of his opinion is a product of his imagination. Few anglers measure their casts or score their accuracy.

Equipment has developed to fit fishing methods. The two most important routes taken by sport fishing in the past 30 years have been toward inshore salt water and to the big artificial impoundments.

Bass, trout and salmon streams have been dammed ever since the colonists erected their waterwheels. Hydroelectric impoundments came on gradually in the early part of the century; they came with a rush with the Tennessee Valley Authority and the overpowering need for more power. The smallmouth rivers of the Ozarks were obliterated, the salmon and steelhead rivers of the Pacific Coast were converted to lakes and desert streams were backed up until black bass fed among drowning cactus. While the new lakes destroyed time-honored ways of fishing, they brought new ones and accommodated more black bass than ever before. Saddened anglers of another era met the fact that fishing for the few was giving way to fishing for the many. Some could not accept the new methods.

Impoundment boom and bust schedules had been known for a long while. In the 30s, biologists began to follow well-documented histories of the lakes. Newly flooded ground was fertile in the things black bass needed and there was invariably a period when the shorelines were crowded with willing fish, even while the lakes were still filling for the first time and a fisherman could look down on green treetops and abandoned game trails.

Dead and dying trees that were flooded were eventually called "stickups" but at first the fishermen didn't pay much attention to underwater ridges, drowned homesteads or one-time highways. They

This Pflueger instrument was one of the first electronic fishfinding instruments available to users of very small boats.

worked the shorelines as they had always worked lake shorelines. After the feast of the first few years came something very much like an angling famine.

A few fishermen who didn't know any better trolled fast and fairly deep and caught some bass despite assurances that they were wasting their time. Some better directed efforts came along, growing popular in the 50s, and the names of Buck Perry and the Spoonplug came with a minor revolution. Perry insisted that only a small percentage of a lake's bass were to be found along the shoreline and that they were there only a small percentage of the time. Veteran shoreline rakers grumbled that the few along the shorelines were the ones they wanted and that Perry could have the rest.

Perry had a way of fishing those bass that had left the shoreline. He used heavy tackle with a metal lure (the Spoonplug) that would dive to the bottom. The tackle was heavy because he trolled very fast and his lure was designed to catch weeds or debris on the bottom and then simply tear loose. It also caught bass and proved that not only were the fish well offshore much of the time but they were concentrated in groups or loose schools, moving or not. When the fish were located, Perry said, you could fish with anything you wanted to as long as it got to the proper depth. His Spoonplug was a fish locator, and after you had found the fish you could put it away if ripping the bottom didn't please you.

Although there had been depthfinders ever since the navy started listening to sonar's eerie pinging for enemy submarines, no one had thought there was any need for them in fresh water. Then there were some experiments with small electronic sound devices. One, a Pflueger model, worked with earphones and a hand-held transducer that enabled the user to hear passing fish or even grass waving in the current.

With the bass boat came inexpensive depth sounders that could detect the presence of shoals of fish, but more importantly could read the "structure" on the bottom of an impoundment. Now the bass angler had something to work with. He secured topographic maps that revealed the exact configuration of a lake, and he could work the bends of an underwater creek bed or fish over what had once been an orchard or a front porch.

Reading "structure" became an all-important skill of the top-notch bass fisherman. He quickly acquired lures to take advantage of his new knowledge. Divers began to spy on the bass. The intense study of black bass began about 1965 and there has never been anything like it.

Second only to the new concept of the way black bass live was the plastic worm, a phenomenon never explained by biologists who are at a loss as to why fish seem to prefer flavors such as licorice and grape.

The idea of a soft, flexible worm is nothing new since there were rubber baits in the 1920s, but those were not especially successful. The final product seems to have grown from various pork rind and leather attractors. Most of the first ones were black.

At first the worms were fished with spinning tackle and were invariably worked gently along the bottom. When a fish took one he was given plenty of time and the rule was never to strike until he had "started to run with it." Later, it developed that the procedure should be varied dependent upon the way the worm was fished and the way the fish acted with it.

From the light spinning rod that threw worms with only a little

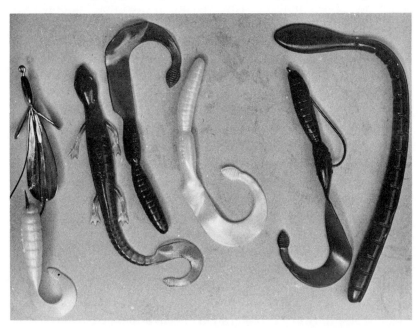

The plain plastic worm, which became recognized as
the best artificial of all time for black bass, had
appeared in a variety of shapes by the 1970s.

weight added, the dedicated worm fisherman graduated to the real "worm rod," which was especially stiff for efficient hook setting, and for the most part the hook setting was somewhat more prompt.

Weedless hooks helped. The "Texas rig," which involved concealing the barb in the worm and using a slip sinker, enabled the lure to be worked through all sorts of obstacles, especially weeds. By that time it was concluded that the worm probably didn't represent any particular bass food but was generally accepted as a creepy, crawly thing that simply had the features of something good to eat. There were even floating worms, light ones that stayed in the surface film and sometimes produced crashing strikes. Comedians remarked that it appeared the bass were designed to go with the worms.

Whether the worm represents a small snake, an unusual eel or simply a plastic worm tasting like licorice or grapes, the accomplished worm fisherman is one of the most skilled practitioners in the angling world. His analysis of the bass' *tap-tap* strike or the more gentle sucking take make him the most effective bass fisherman ever, and if he is also skilled in the spinnerbait and the crankbait he is ready for a bass tournament. All he needs is a topo map of the lake, a depth finder to read structure, a thermometer and instruments for testing oxygen content and clarity. Given his black bass fishing credentials he becomes a fairly deadly pike or walleye fisherman, and should do well with striped bass too.

A great many investigators observed bass with scuba equipment. Jerry Gibbs, fishing editor of *Outdoor Life*, did it for long periods and if his written observations didn't make his readers better fishermen they certainly gave them all of the necessary elements. Glen Lau, the outdoor movie producer, was another bass spy of note, using glass-sided tanks as well as fishing-scene study. Only underwater observation showed the actual ways in which the bass struck the lure. Some of the revelations seemed incredible; one of the most startling concerned the use of "crankbaits" at high speed.

Fast-reeled lures, it had been believed, were perfect for hooking striking fish. Unlike the gently manipulated surface or bottom bait that the fish could taste and reject gently, it was thought that the fast-moving lure indicated strikes instantly and the fish generally hooked himself. But underwater observation revealed that a very large bass could cruise up to a fast-moving crankbait, take it into his mouth and then reject it while the fisherman never knew he'd had a strike—if such a sampling can be called that.

While the plastic worm was used in a variety of ways from top to bottom, the new school of bass fishermen who could detect all sorts of things through their sensitive rod tips found new ways of using baits intended for other methods. They took advantage of some fish senses we hadn't been sure of. For example, on some occasions a spinnerbait would catch fish when nudged along the bottom in muddy water. Those who made it work explained that no fish could see much under such conditions but that the fish's hearing or vibration detection (about the same thing) would lead it to a clicking thing if it were near enough to his nose.

Some California bass fishermen used a method called "flipping" in some weedy lakes and took it to prestigious tournaments, where it became part of the professional bass fisherman's bag of tricks. Within a few months there were specially made flipping rods.

The system involves an overly long spinning rod that is used to lower a lure through small openings in the weeds or brush. Slight lateral movement with some up-and-down operation has been quite

Bass boats grew larger and hurried more and more.
This Ranger for 1981 is rated for 175 horsepower.
(Photo from Wood Manufacturing Co. Inc.)

successful. For that matter, tournament entrants had been lowering their lures straight down into dead treetops for some time. One of them insisted that cold weather was an especially good time to get a bait "low and slow" next to a big submerged tree trunk.

"Everybody knows," he said, "that decaying vegetable matter gives off heat. The fish are there to keep warm."

While most fishermen doubted that a slowly rotting tree could warm a bass very much, they had no argument with the fact that the fish were there.

Faced with the necessity of catching bass under adverse conditions, the "cast-for-cash" people concluded that although bass were sluggish and consumed little food during very cold or very hot periods, they could be made to take an occasional lure if it were worked slowly and close to their noses. Part of this was the "new science" and part of it was the necessity for producing under adverse conditions—a certain mother of invention.

Some new techniques helped the light-tackle saltwater fisherman. Some of the most impressive catches were made in shallow water, beginning in the 1950s. New baitcasting reels with efficient drags and the spinning outfits were hard on almost any fish that couldn't go to great depths. Heavy-duty fly reels could handle almost anything the rod and leader would hold and had enough capacity for long runs, at least giving the boatman time to follow. It was found that tarpon flies needn't be quite as big as formerly supposed, and there were some huge "sailfish poppers" of styrofoam that could be cast pretty well with fly rods. And there were new systems in teasers and chumming.

If a fisherman wants to hook a big offshore fish with very light tackle, there is a system of trolling teasers and then showing him the hooked lure when his appetite has been whetted. Sometimes it has been a three-stage approach: the fish would be attracted by a trolled teaser, then a hookless surface plug on a heavy outfit would be used—then the lure with the hook would be presented to a fish ready to strike almost anything that moved. Admittedly, some of this is not exactly a purist's approach, but the fish fight just as hard as if there was only one bait.

Chumming became an art in many depths of water. Off Bermuda there is a special system of delivering chum to tidal currents from a charter boat, the chum being released both at the surface and from a

*Using typical light-tipped casting rod,
a British Columbia angler plays a big steelhead caught
on a bobber-type lure.*

submerged basket, and an excited angler may be startled at the things which appear off the stern. While many fishermen might feel the water is too deep for chumming there, they might be equally surprised at chumming in inches of water as done by some of the top bonefish guides.

Some bonefishermen were pleased at the results achieved by Bahama natives many years ago, but Florida guides such as Bill Curtis of Miami have it to a science. Curtis, who operates mainly in Biscayne Bay in sight of Miami Beach's pastel skyline, has been tutor for a number of younger guides of excellent reputation. He chooses a light spot on the bottom where he knows bonefish are likely to travel and baits it with a double handful of diced shrimp. He and his client then simply watch for the customers to appear, certainly a simplification of the hunting procedure usually applied to bonefish.

Some of the less glamorous quarry, such as bluegills, crappies and other sunfishes have achieved more of a standing as gamefish with the advancement of spinning tackle. The jig became a potent lure, especially for crappie. Fishermen worked near brushpiles and submerged "structure" with a gentle up-and-down retrieve, often bumping the bottom, and learned the subtle feel as the jig stops on one of the dropbacks or draws a plucking strike on the way up.

Along with small panfish jigs came some ultra-light lures that had been an abomination with fly rods but went well with spinning gear, using line of 4-pound test or less. These worked with some miniature pushbutton reels and matching rods, sold as combinations, and were quite capable of handling an occasional bass or pike. By the 80s there were some effective miniature spinnerbaits, some of them weighing about a tenth of an ounce.

Trout fishermen became better, in their way as skilled as the bass fishermen, and much of their improvement was due to advanced study of entomology and a willingness (to the disgust of some traditionalists) to use nymphs and streamers near the bottom. The difference in trout fishing expertise between 1955 and 1975 was enormous and there was a sudden widespread acceptance of the catch-and-release ethic.

Since there were greatly increased numbers of anglers the meat fisherman was in growing disfavor. It was a surprise to many to find by the late 70s a concentration of good fishermen on catch-and-release waters which had been almost lonely a few years before. This

*Angler using casting tackle lands a steelhead caught
with a bobber-type lure and pencil sinker.*

made the fish harder to catch but didn't reduce their numbers. Fish managers were delighted and spoke of the "fishing experience" instead of the full creel.

Sinking lines of various densities, from "slow sinkers" to those carrying names such as "Deep Water Express," made it possible for trout fishermen to work at almost any depth they could cast to. Late fall brown trout fishing became almost a new sport with sinking lines, as fishermen temporarily abandoned their tiny dries and dainty nymphs for big streamers and really big fish.

Steelhead had attracted fly fishermen from the 20s on but it had been a sometime thing until the deep-going lines. With sinking heads fly fishermen could take the winter run fish, formerly available only to other tackle.

A special school of elite steelheaders used their long casting rods with the sensitive tips to work pencil sinkers that bumped the bottom. The sinker could be trimmed to fit the current and the lures were offshoots of the Cherry Bobber, which had revolutionized steelheading for casters. What did it represent? Possibly salmon eggs, a rainbow trout delicacy.

What had once been known as "technical trout water" became more and more valuable as fishermen began to accept the premise that in the end the most difficult fish were the most valuable. When Dermot Wilson acquired fishing rights on the Test and Itchen Rivers in England and offered anglers fishing for pay by the day his enterprise was welcomed with enthusiasm. Salmon rivers had been very expensive for many years. American "spring creeks" as they were called in the West and "limestone streams" as they were known in the East suddenly posed access problems. If left wide open to public fishing they could not accommodate the new throngs of trout fishermen. Some of the owners began to charge by the day, a business that brought cries of disapproval at first, but eventually was seen as the solution to a difficult problem.

The stream owner who charged anglers and controlled his water could keep the attendance within reason, and since his stream provided part of his income he had an added incentive to improve it and to study the trout's welfare.

Fishermen don't always take advantage of available fishing, and in some cases biology outdistances the casters. The striped bass, pursued with almost every conceivable form of tackle at one time or

*The late Joe Cather, designer of the tiny spoons that
trim his hat, helped to popularize shad fishing.*

another, appears as a different fish in different waters, ranging from fairly swift rivers to deep impoundments. There is some confusion regarding origins when natural stocks are supplemented by hatchery fish, and migrations are hard to follow, so striped bass fishermen of the 80s are doing a bit of pioneering.

Some species and methods have been ignored until recent years. The American shad had been a prized gamefish on the North Atlantic coast for a long time before it was transplanted to California. On West Coast rivers fly fishermen have been enjoying the shad for a long time, even though a few of them use the term "stink salmon." Their tactics are about the same as those for steelhead.

There was no need to introduce shad to Florida. Apparently they have been operating there as long as they have been farther north but no one seemed to pay any attention to them as a gamefish until the 1940s, when a widely-traveled fisherman named Norton Webster settled on a fly rod, fly reel and monofilament line for slow trolling on the St. Johns River. He also caught shad by casting with spinning tackle, using a variety of small, shiny lures. Shad fishing became a family sport, with all sorts of boats patrolling the known concentration stretches of the slow-moving river.

A number of lures originated especially for the trolling job, notably the little Cather spoon, which worked on northern shad too. Joe Cather, originator of the spoons, preferred Webster's method of trolling, using monofilament line and various combinations of his spoons with little jigs or "darts."

Florida has never had very many fly fishermen. It may be that I originated true fly fishing for Florida shad in the 60s; but having repeatedly researched fishing methods that caught on several generations after their earliest practitioners had been ignored, I suspect I'm simply the first to make noise about it.

I first tried using Cather's little spoons on a fly rod but the things were abominable to cast, so I enlisted Ray Donnersberger, a confirmed fly inventor. We caught some shad with his creations using sinking fly lines, and we developed a technique that certainly wasn't new, but simply an adaptation of steelhead methods, altered to fit the slowly moving St. Johns. A persistent fly-fishing biologist named Forrest Ware took it to more advanced stages.

I wrote about our adventures and although it took almost 15 years from my beginning I am now receiving frequent inquiries from fly fishermen headed to Florida. This story is not entirely an ego trip. I just want to point out the way new fishing methods get started and how they can lag for long periods.

When sport fishing entered the 1980s it came with more fishermen than ever before, but with a growing knowledge of gamefish, and the realization that if we were to have enough in the future they would have to be caught more than once.

BIBLIOGRAPHY

Babson, Stanley M., *Bonefishing*. New York, Winchester Press, rev. ed., 1973

Barnes, George W., *How to Make Bamboo Fly Rods*. New York, Winchester Press, 1977.

Bates, Joseph D., Jr., *Streamers and Bucktails, the Big Fish Flies*. New York, Alfred A. Knopf, 1979.

Bethune, George Washington, ed., *The Compleat Angler*. American edition, 1847.

Brooks, Joe, *Trout Fishing*. New York, Harper & Row, 1972.

Brown, John J., *American Angler's Guide*. New York, Appleton, 1876.

Chase, Mary Ellen, *The Fishing Fleets of New England*. Boston, Houghton Mifflin, 1961.

Dablemont, Larry, *The Authentic American Johnboat*. New York, David McKay Co., Inc., 1978.

Dimock, A.W., *Book of the Tarpon*. London, 1912.

Drucker, Philip, *Indians of the Northwest Coast*. Garden City, New York, Natural History, 1963.

Farrington, Kip, Jr., *Fishing the Pacific*. New York, Van Rees Press, 1953.

Forester, Frank (Henry William Herbert), *The Complete Manual For Young Sportsmen*. New York, George E. Woodward, 1856.

Gabrielson, Ira N., and LaMonte, Francesca, *The New Fisherman's Encyclopedia*. Harrisburg, PA, Stackpole, 1950.

Gemming, Elizabeth, *Blow Ye Winds Westerly.* New York, Crowell, 1971.

Gifford, Tommy, *Anglers and Muscleheads.* New York, Dutton, 1960.

Gingrich, Arnold, *The Fishing in Print.* New York, Winchester Press, 1974.

Gresham, Grits, *Complete Book of Bass Fishing.* New York, Outdoor Life, Harper & Row, 1966.

Grey, Zane, *Tales of Fishes.* New York, Harper, 1919.

Halford, Frederic, *Floating Flies and How to Dress Them.* 1886.

Heacox, Cecil E., *The Compleat Brown Trout.* New York, Winchester Press, 1974.

Henshall, Dr. James A., Bass, *Pike Perch & Other Game Fishes of North America.* Cincinnati, 1919.

——————————— *Book of the Black Bass.* Cincinnati, Clarke, 1904.

Hewitt, E.R., *A Trout and Salmon Fisherman for Seventy-five Years.* New York, Abercrombie & Fitch, Ann Arbor MI, University Microfilms, 1966.

Hills, John Waller, *A History of Fly Fishing For Trout.* 1921, Rockville, NY, Freshet Press ed., 1971.

Holder, Charles Frederick, *The Log of a Sea Angler.* Boston, Houghton Mifflin, 1906

Hurum, Hans Jorgen, *A History of the Fish Hook.* New York, Winchester Press, 1976.

Karas, Nicholas, *The Complete Book of the Striped Bass.* New York, Winchester Press, 1974

Keane, Martin J., *Classic Rods and Rodmakers.* New York, Winchester Press, 1976.

Koller, Larry, *The Treasury of Angling.* New York, Ridge/Golden, 1963.

LaFarge, Oliver, *A Pictorial History of the American Indian.* New York, Crown, 1956.

Livingston, A.D., *Fishing For Bass.* New York & Philadelphia, Lippencott, 1974.

Lyman, Henry, *Bluefishing.* New York, Barnes, 1955.

——————————, *The Complete Book of Bluefishing.* New York, Barnes, 1959.

——————————— and Woolner, Frank, *The Complete Book of Striped Bass Fishing.* New York, Barnes, 1954.

Luckey, Carl F., *Old Fishing Lures and Tackle.* Florence, AL, Books Americana, Inc.

Bibliography

Marinaro, Vincent, *A Modern Dry Fly Code*. New York, Crown, 1950.

McClane, A.J., *McClane's Standard Fishing Encyclopedia*. New York, Holt, Rinehart and Winston, 1974.

McDonald, John, *Quill Gordon*. New York, Knopf, 1972.

Melner, Samuel, and Kessler, Hermann, *Great Fishing Tackle Catalogs of the Golden Age*. New York, Crown, 1972.

Migdalski, Edward C., *Angler's Guide to the Fresh Water Sport Fishes of North America*. New York, Ronald, 1962.

Miles, Charles, *Indian and Eskimo Artifacts of North America*. Chicago, Regnery, 1963.

Moser, Commander Jefferson F., *Alaska Salmon and Salmon Fisheries*. Washington, DC, Government Printing Office, 1899.

Moss, Frank T., *Successful Striped Bass Fishing*. Camden, ME, International Marine, 1974.

Needham, Paul, *Trout Streams*. New York, Winchester Press, 1969.

Netboy, Anthony, *The Atlantic Salmon, A Vanishing Species?*. London, Faber and Faber, 1968.

———————————— *Salmon of the Pacific Northwest*. Portland, OR, Metropolitan, 1958.

Norris, Thaddeus, *The American Angler's Book*. Philadelphia, Porter & Coates, 1864.

Reiger, George, *Profiles in Salt Water Angling*. Englewood Cliffs, NJ, Prentice-Hall, 1973.

Reinfelder, Al, *Bait Tail Fishing*. New York, Barnes, 1969.

Ritz, Charles, *A Fly Fisher's Life*. New York, Winchester Press, 1969.

Roosevelt, Robert B., *Superior Fishing*. New York, Carleton, 1865.

St. John, Larry, *Practical Bait Casting*. New York, Macmillan, 1920.

———————————— *Practical Fly Fishing*. New York, Macmillan, 1923.

Salter, T.F., *The Angler's Guide*. London, Carpenter, 1823.

Scott, Genio C., *Fishing In American Waters*. New York, Harper, 1869.

Skues, G.E.M., *Nymph Fishing For Chalk Stream Trout*. London, 1939.

Trench, Charles Chenevix, *A History of Angling*. Chicago, Follett, 1974.

Walker, C.F., *The Art of Chalk Stream Fishing*. Harrisburg, PA, Stackpole, 1968.

Waterman, Charles F., *Fishing In America*. New York, Ridge/Holt, Rinehart & Winston, New York, 1975.

Woolner, Frank, *Modern Saltwater Sport Fishing*. New York, Crown, 1972.

Wulff, Lee, *The Atlantic Salmon*. New York, Barnes, 1958.

INDEX

Index